GARY LADD

Saguaro cactuses cling to a sun-tinted hillside in Arizona as the Sonoran Desert cools at moonrise.

In the outback of Australia, Ayers Rock weathers the centuries.

The

*Prepared by the Special Publications Division
National Geographic Society, Washington, D.C.*

GEORG GERSTER

Desert Realm

Lands of Majesty and Mystery

THE DESERT REALM

Contributing Authors
TOR EIGELAND, DR. FAROUK EL-BAZ, LOREN MCINTYRE,
    TOM MELHAM, THOMAS O'NEILL, JOYCE STEWART

Contributing Photographers
JIN BOHONG, TOR EIGELAND, GEORG GERSTER,
    ETHAN HOFFMAN, LOREN MCINTYRE, JAMES L. STANFIELD

Published by The National Geographic Society
GILBERT M. GROSVENOR, *President*
MELVIN M. PAYNE, *Chairman of the Board*
OWEN R. ANDERSON, *Executive Vice President*
ROBERT L. BREEDEN, *Vice President, Publications
    and Educational Media*

Prepared by The Special Publications Division
DONALD J. CRUMP, *Editor*
PHILIP B. SILCOTT, *Associate Editor*
WILLIAM L. ALLEN, WILLIAM R. GRAY, *Senior Editors*

Staff for this book
RICHARD M. CRUM, *Managing Editor*
RALPH GRAY, *Contributing Editor*
DENNIS R. DIMICK, *Picture Editor*
JOSEPHINE B. BOLT, *Art Director*
KATHLEEN F. TETER, *Senior Researcher and Assistant
    to the Editor*
PENELOPE DIAMANTI DE WIDT, *Senior Researcher*
MONIQUE F. EINHORN, JANE L. MATTESON, *Researchers*
KATHRYN P. INGRAHAM, MARGARET V. WALKINSHAW,
    Research Assistants

Illustrations and Design
CYNTHIA B. SCUDDER, *Assistant to the Art Director*
MARIANNE R. KOSZORUS, CINDA ROSE, *Assistant Designers*
JANET DYER, D. RANDY YOUNG, *Design Assistants*
CAROL A. ROCHELEAU, *Illustrations Assistant*
JOHN D. GARST, JR., PETER BALCH, GARY M. JOHNSON,
    JOSEPH F. OCHLAK, MARK SEIDLER, JUDITH BELL SIEGEL,
    Map Research, Design, and Production
PAMELA A. BLACK, JANE H. BUXTON, TONI EUGENE,
    KAREN M. KOSTYAL, CHRISTINE ECKSTROM LEE,
    TOM MELHAM, H. ROBERT MORRISON, LISA A. OLSON,
    THOMAS O'NEILL, DAN SPERLING, SUZANNE VENINO,
    Picture Legend Writers

Engraving, Printing, and Product Manufacture
ROBERT W. MESSER, *Manager*
GEORGE V. WHITE, *Production Manager*
RAJA D. MURSHED, DAVID V. SHOWERS, *Project Managers*
MARK R. DUNLEVY, RICHARD A. MCCLURE,
    GREGORY STORER, *Assistant Production Managers*
KATHERINE H. DONOHUE, *Senior Production Assistant*
MARY A. BENNETT, KATHERINE R. LEITCH,
    Production Staff Assistants

NANCY F. BERRY, PAMELA A. BLACK, NETTIE BURKE,
    MARY ELIZABETH DAVIS, CLAIRE M. DOIG, ROSAMUND GARNER,
    VICTORIA D. GARRETT, MARY JANE GORE, JANE R. HALPIN,
    NANCY J. HARVEY, SHERYL A. HOEY, JOAN HURST,
    ARTEMIS S. LAMPATHAKIS, VIRGINIA A. MCCOY,
    MERRICK P. MURDOCK, CLEO PETROFF, VICTORIA I. PISCOPO,
    TAMMY PRESLEY, KATHERYN M. SLOCUM, JENNY TAKACS,
    Staff Assistants

JEFFREY A. BROWN, *Index*

Copyright © 1982 National Geographic Society. All rights
reserved. Reproduction of the whole or any part of the contents
without written permission is prohibited.
Library of Congress CIP Data: page 304.

HARDCOVER: A SATELLITE IMAGE CAPTURES A REMOTE CORNER OF THE
DUNE-DAPPLED RUB AL-KHALI ON THE ARABIAN PENINSULA.
GEOPIC IMAGES/EARTH SATELLITE CORPORATION

DR. HANS RITTER

"Whatever causes diversity ... on the surface of our planet,— mountains, great lakes, grassy steppes, and even deserts ... impresses some peculiar mark or character on ... its inhabitants," wrote South American explorer and scientist Alexander von Humboldt in the 1800s. In North Africa a Tuareg salt trader (left) bears the "mark" of the Sahara, a robe and veil worn as protection against blowing sand and glaring sun.

LOREN MCINTYRE

Deserts in a New Light:
      An Introduction   8

The Great Basin, Sonoran, Mojave,
            and Chihuahuan of North America   44

Along South America's West Coast   76

The Sahara of North Africa   110

Southern Africa's Kalahari and Namib   148

The Middle East   184

Asia's Taklimakan and Gobi   218

The Outback of Australia   248

Secrets of Living in Arid Lands   284

Notes on Contributors   300

Acknowledgments   300

Additional Reading   300

Index   301

*Stronghold of the Inca civilization, the Andes
guard 500-year-old ruins preserved by the
extreme dryness of Peru's desert air.*

Stark Worlds of Hidden Beauty

Deserts of the Earth in a New Light

Introduction by
Dr. Faroūk El-Baz

Rippled by dunes, a sand sea in
the Sahara swells beyond Lake
Mandara in Libya. Though
plagued by aridity, the world's
dry regions offer the allure of
palm-fringed oases, bright
seasonal flowers, resourceful
animals, persevering peoples,
and awesome landforms.

UWE GEORGE/GEO MAGAZINE

"**H**assan!" I called out to my colleague from Cairo's Ain Shams University. "Wake up or you will miss the sunrise."

"*Sabah el-kheir.*" Uttering this "good morning," Hassan sat up in his sleeping bag and for some time did not move or speak another word. His attention was held by the spectacle about to burst across the Farafra depression, 300 miles southwest of Cairo in the heart of Egypt's Western Desert.

Standing barefoot in the cool sand, I studied the cloudless horizon, where a pale blue ribbon separated the earth from the night sky. It was early fall, the air clear, the surroundings profoundly still. The only sound was that of the whispering wind. A faint aroma of clay, the characteristic scent of this corner of Africa's vast Sahara, drifted in the air.

Suddenly, an arc of the glowing sun sprang from the horizon. Soft rays gradually accentuated distant escarpments and hillsides. As the sun rose higher, its light breathed life into the soft texture of the white, wind-sculpted pillars around me. The progression of the rays spread across the carpet of sand and illuminated the desert floor with brilliance.

For me, one sunrise in the desert is worth a thousand in humid regions. An arid land's lack of vegetation allows rocks and soils to display their textures in subtle hues, changing with each hour of the day.

"Every sunrise in the desert is different, and this one is especially eerie," exclaimed photographer Georg Gerster. He had accompanied my field party into the Farafra depression, where we were conducting a geological study of wind-eroded rocks. "These white rocks look to me like icebergs at the edge of Antarctica," he said.

Georg was right. The chalky limestone blocks and pillars around us did look like giant chunks of floating ice. These rocks are remnants of a thick layer deposited in oceans of the geological past, some 65 million years ago. Later, the ocean floor was uplifted and its water receded, leaving a vast high plain. Running surface water from rainfall eroded the rock, slicing deep valleys into its surface. When the climate became drier, the desert was born, and the exposed rock succumbed to the sharp cutting edge of the wind.

Similar geologic and climatic changes have created many hyperarid, arid, and semiarid regions in the world. These tracts make up one-third of the earth's landmasses. The hot deserts exist in two separate belts. One band girds the earth around the Tropic of Cancer, the other around the Tropic of Capricorn. Here, between latitudes 15° and 30° north and south of the Equator, deserts exist on every continent except Europe, although relatively dry parts lie in southern Spain. In contrast to the hot deserts, where daytime temperatures have climbed to a blistering 136°F, are the cold deserts. These areas cover ten million square miles in regions of the Arctic and the Antarctic. Polar desert temperatures in most places seldom exceed 50°F and can drop to minus 95°F.

Few people have ventured into the heart of the world's deserts, and many of those who have dared did not stay long. Some who remained, however, established cultures that ultimately influenced life-styles in lands around the world. Out of the arid wastes of the Arabian Desert, for instance, arose a sturdy and tough people, the Arabs. In the seventh century they ventured from their environment to spread Islam. Eventually their rich cultural heritage extended from Spain to China. In the 13th century Genghis Khan and his hordes rode

Mud-brick minaret of a 17th-century Egyptian mosque in El Qasr emphasizes the architectural style that dominates many desert villages (opposite). Below: Like generations of oasis dwellers before her, a woman in Egypt's Western Desert carries water in clay jugs. In a mural from an Egyptian tomb, a farmer harvests grain by hand (bottom). Today ancient agricultural methods continue little changed in some of the world's arid lands.

GEORG GERSTER (ALL)

14

ascending moist currents into frothy, billowing clouds. As the clouds climb to loftier altitudes, their moisture cools and condenses into droplets, and beads of rain fall to earth.

Most tropical clouds burst into precipitation near the Equator between latitudes 15° North and 15° South. The resulting heavy rains not only account for the lush tropical forests, but they also foreshadow the aridity of the lands lying in higher latitudes. The same air mass that soaked the rain forests now contains little moisture. Winds force the cool air downward, and as it circulates back toward the earth's surface it warms up again. This descending dry air becomes a hot breath blowing across landmasses that straddle the Tropic of Cancer and the Tropic of Capricorn. Consequently, in these rainless belts exist some of the world's most arid lands: the Sahara of northern Africa, the Arabian Desert, and the Namib Desert of southern Africa.

One of nature's greatest paradoxes is that a region lying next to an ocean can be a desert. This phenomenon occurs because ocean currents play a role in climate. The fog-banked deserts of South America and southern Africa, for instance, owe their existence largely to cold ocean currents flowing from the direction of Antarctica toward the Equator. The Peru Current streams along South America's west coast off the Atacama and Peruvian Deserts. The Benguela Current sweeps past the Namib Desert on the southwestern edge of Africa. The cool water of these currents brushing against warm coastal air throws off blankets of fog, which trap moisture at the surface level and prevent the moist air from rising to form rain clouds. Nevertheless, moisture from a fog can quench aridity. But another force intervenes: the wind. Breezes along the western fringes of South America and southern Africa flow parallel with the coast. The southerly wind holds the fog near the shore; little moisture reaches the land where deserts reign.

Distance from oceans that feed moisture into air streams can also create arid regions. Many lands in central Asia receive scant rainfall because their wind systems have lost almost all moisture to other terrain during a long overland journey. Such inland deserts include the Gobi of China and the Mongolian People's Republic, and the Turkestan of the Soviet Union. Mountains too may cause aridity, mainly in areas called rain-shadow deserts. The high mountains serve as barriers that force landward streams of warm moist air into higher, cooler altitudes. The gradual change in air temperature triggers condensation, and rain spills on the mountain heights. The air mass, no longer laden with moisture, continues to rise, crosses the mountain peaks, and makes an arid sweep down the other side of the range. Here in the dry shadow of the rain, deserts exist—such as the Patagonian Desert in the lee of the Andes on the east coast of South America and in some highland regions on the west coast, such as the Altiplano of Peru and Bolivia.

Dryness, the essence of the desert, can be measured by aridity indexes. One such scale shows the ratio of radiant energy to annual precipitation at the land surface. The index reads like a reverse rain gauge: the higher the number, the drier the desert. Highest and driest—with a top rating of 200—are the eastern Sahara and a part of the Atacama and Peruvian Deserts. Solar radiation striking these tracts and radiation from the earth *(Continued on page 21)*

ASIA

EUROPE

GOBI

TURKESTAN
DESERT

TAKLIMAKAN
DESERT

DASHT-E KAVIR

WESTERN
DESERT

GREAT INDIAN
DESERT

SAHARA

ARABIAN
DESERT

PACIFIC
OCEAN

RUB AL-KHALI

SOMALI-CHALBI
DESERT

AFRICA

INDIAN
OCEAN

GREAT SANDY
DESERT

NAMIB
DESERT

GIBSON
DESERT

SIMPSON
DESERT

KALAHARI
DESERT

GREAT VICTORIA
DESERT

AUSTRALIA

ATLANTIC
OCEAN

ARCTIC OCEAN

North
Pole

ANTARCTICA
South
Pole

PACIFIC
OCEAN

60°N

60°S

13

forth from the edge of the Gobi in Mongolia. The Mongols carved out an enormous empire from the Pacific Ocean westward to the Black Sea.

Each of the world's dry tracts has fostered wild speculation and superstitions. In the grapevine-shaded oasis of Turpan in Xinjiang, the northwestern-most region of the People's Republic of China, I have heard Muslim Uygurs warn travelers about demons and devils in the dreaded wasteland beyond their haven. The fabled mystique of the desert; the grandeur of arid lands; the ability of plants, animals, and humans to adapt to a severe environment; the advancement of new knowledge about the hyperarid, arid, and semiarid lands of the earth—these subjects have inspired the publication of *The Desert Realm: Lands of Majesty and Mystery.*

In many cases more knowledge exists about mountain ranges, lush river basins, and even glacial terrains than about arid lands. To better understand the desert, I have been working with a new tool—space imagery. Images recorded by Landsat—unmanned satellites—bare secrets of the geological history of dry regions. Throughout this book, pictures produced from Landsat images provide readers with a fresh and colorful view of a stark realm.

What created this harsh environment called the desert? The answer is simple. Land turns into desert because of scarcity of rain or the complete lack of it. Most experts agree that a desert is a land area that receives less than ten inches of precipitation a year. Some desert areas record more rainfall, but it comes sporadically; some moisture soaks in, but most of it runs off or evaporates.

Not long ago, I visited a meteorological station in Siwa Oasis in northwestern Egypt. Here weather information has been gathered since the early 1940s. The chief meteorologist, a local tribesman trained by the British, escorted me to a battery of instruments that measured wind velocity and direction, barometric pressure, temperature, humidity, and the rate of water loss to the dry atmosphere. One instrument was concentrating beams of sunshine through a lens onto a strip of cardboard marked to indicate the hours of the day. If the sun disappeared behind a cloud, the exact time would be recorded on the paper strip. I looked for notations of clouds, which one would expect to find in a place only 150 miles from the Mediterranean seashore. The exposed trail of paper, however, showed only perpetual sunshine.

"How much rain has fallen during the past year?" I asked.

My host answered simply, "Zero."

When and where rain falls depends on the circulation of earth's atmosphere, a complex system that involves evaporation, condensation, and wind and ocean currents. Regions lying along the earth's Equator receive more direct sunlight for longer periods each day than do any other geographical areas. In this equatorial zone, heated air picks up moisture from the evaporation of large amounts of ocean surface water. Moist warm air expands like an invisible balloon. Rising to higher levels in the atmosphere, it leaves behind a zone of reduced air pressure at the earth's surface.

Into this low-pressure area rushes cooler, heavier air, so reliable in its east-west flow that sailors of wind-driven trading ships named the breezes the trade winds. The air currents circulating into the low-pressure zone push the rising warm-air mass even higher and spin the *(Continued on page 14)*

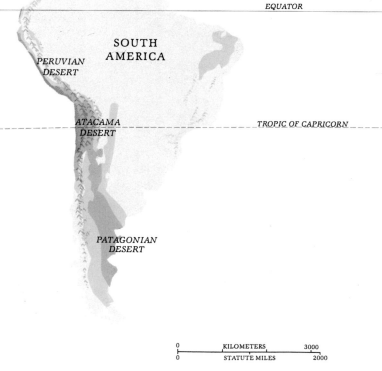

NORTH
AMERICA

ATLANTIC
OCEAN

GREAT
BASIN

MOJAVE
DESERT

SONORAN
DESERT

PACIFIC
OCEAN

CHIHUAHUAN
DESERT

TROPIC OF CANCER

EQUATOR

SOUTH
AMERICA

PERUVIAN
DESERT

ATACAMA
DESERT

TROPIC OF CAPRICORN

PATAGONIAN
DESERT

*C*orridors of aridity, girdling the globe around the
Tropic of Cancer and the Tropic of Capricorn, create
deserts and zones less parched but still rain-poor (see
key below). These two major dry belts owe their
existence to hot air that rises at the Equator, sheds rain
in the tropics, and moves toward the poles only to
descend void of moisture in subtropical latitudes. Arid
conditions worldwide stem from many causes, including
temperature inversions that inhibit the formation of
rain clouds, high-rising mountains that rob moisture
from clouds drifting inland, and isolated continental
interiors that lie far from the reach of moist air masses.
Scant precipitation makes parts of the polar regions
(insets) as arid as the more familiar hot deserts of lower
latitudes. Dry lands, including ten million square miles
of polar deserts, cover one-third of the earth, touch
every continent, and support nearly a billion people.

Hyperarid
Arid
Semiarid

KILOMETERS
0   3000
0   2000
STATUTE MILES

Waging war against sand: Workers plant cactuses and casuarina trees in an effort to halt spreading dunes that threaten a seaport in Somalia. At the dune-control project in Somalia, rows of thorny casuarina protect beds of sand-stabilizing cactuses from roaming goats and cows (opposite). The battle against the dunes has tamed thousands of windblown acres in the Somali-Chalbi Desert. Many desert nations fight encroaching dunes. In Egypt and China, waves of sand have engulfed roads and even entire villages.

MIKE YAMASHITA/WOODFIN CAMP & ASSOCIATES (BOTH)

*G*raceful as a dancer, a herdsman (below) in the Great Indian Desert winds his 14-yard-long cotton turban after washing it in a nearby well. The headdress shields him from the sun and from temperatures that can climb as high as 125°F. A thatch roof aids air circulation in one of the region's desert huts (above). Bright robes, bracelets, and rings make up the festive finery of a mother and child in arid northwest India (opposite).

GEORG GERSTER (ALL)

have the power to evaporate 200 times the amount of received precipitation. By contrast, the ratio stands at 50 or less for the western Sahara and areas of the Arabian Desert, and 10 for the northwest corner of the Sonoran Desert, one of the driest regions in the United States.

Natural and man-made hazards to travel in hyperarid tracts reinforce the perception in many people's minds that deserts are hostile. The treacherous salt crust caking the surface of quicksand-like marshes in the Dasht-e Kavir, or Salt Desert, of north-central Iran can give way and bog down travelers. Land mines left by World War II armies in the sand near the Qattara Depression in northern Egypt also pose dangers to wayfarers. It's the vision of burning sand, however, stretching for miles to the horizon and beyond that has discouraged many desert explorers.

"**S**and dunes with sand between, an ocean of sand, this was the one thing that might make any farther advance impossible for us. Any other hindrances could have been overcome. Mountains could have been climbed. . . . There could be no fear whatever of hostile dwellers in an area bare of all human beings or living creatures . . . but an unbroken sandy sea brought everything to naught. . . ." These mournful words were written by German explorer Gerhard Rohlfs in the late 19th century, after he had explored the Great Sand Sea in the eastern Sahara.

An even bigger domain of dunes is the Rub al-Khali, the Empty Quarter, in the Arabian Peninsula. This desert, the world's largest ocean of sand, swells with steep dunes more than 800 feet high and spreads across 250,000 square miles, an area about the size of Texas. The Rub al-Khali's temperature has been recorded at 122°F in the summer and 41°F in the winter. The inaccessibility of the mysterious region nurtured legends of walled cities and flourishing demons. Only an airship could cross it, observed T. E. Lawrence (Lawrence of Arabia) in 1929. A couple of years later two Englishmen, Bertram Thomas and H. St. John B. Philby, guided by Bedouin in separate journeys into the Rub al-Khali, became the first Westerners to cross "the veritable desert."

About the same time, British army officer Ralph Bagnold ventured into Egypt's Western Desert, then called the Libyan Desert, "among the ruins of desert kingdoms and the crocks and querns of prehistoric tribes; beyond . . . the last bone of man or of mouse; in places where nothing exists, no sprouting grassblade nor worm of decay; where perhaps, in certain spots, nothing ever did exist."

Bagnold replaced the traditional desert conveyance, the camel, with the most modern ground transportation of his time, the Model T Ford and later the Model A. Trucks were also used. Once, at the edge of Egypt's Great Sand Sea, Bagnold found himself in a truck facing a huge dune rampart.

"Soon another bank of yellow loomed up ahead continuous, smooth and featureless, an uncertain distance away," he later wrote. "Should we attempt to cross it? I increased speed to forty miles an hour, feeling like a small boy on a horse about to take his first big fence. . . . A huge glaring wall of yellow shot up high into the sky a yard in front of us. The lorry tipped violently backwards— and we rose as in a lift, smoothly without vibration. We floated up and up on a yellow cloud. All the accustomed car movements had ceased; only the

New view of deserts: Muted tones shade semiarid regions in this image of the Great Indian Desert taken from space (opposite). The city of Jaipur appears as a black spot at lower center. Blue indicates water. The white patch at lower left marks a nearly dry salt lake. Waterless rivers form a network of white veins. Red means vegetation, the deepest hue being the forested Aravalli Range. Composites such as this one come from data collected by Landsat. The orbiting satellites scan the earth's surface and record reflected light waves, which computers translate into images. Landsat portraits aid the study of desert landforms and the search for groundwater, minerals, and other resources.

GEOPIC IMAGES/EARTH SATELLITE CORPORATION

speedometer told us we were still moving fast. It was incredible." Bagnold today marvels that machines can now lift desert explorers above the dunes and literally out of the world. In orbit hundreds of miles above earth, astronauts can clearly observe and photograph the world's arid landforms. From their findings, the direction of sand-dune movement can be charted. Knowing the direction of dunes proves valuable at the edge of the desert, where shifting sands present a hazard to human habitation. Furthermore, photographs from space depict a desert's color variations, which indicate changes in soil composition, particularly the reddening of sand as it migrates from its source.

"Close to the Mediterranean, desert colors seem to be fairly light. But some of the material we saw in the central part was more reddish," reported Astronaut D. K. (Deke) Slayton, after orbiting above the Sahara during the Apollo-Soyuz mission in 1975.

Similarly, photographs taken by Skylab astronauts of the Namib Desert on the southwestern coast of Africa showed that the red color in its dunes became more intense as distance increased inland from the coast. This reddening, primarily associated with age, comes from clay and iron oxide that coat individual sand grains. My research team has discovered that in parts of the Western Desert in Egypt the coating thickens, causing a deeper red color in the sand. This knowledge allows us to use the intensity of red color as an indicator of the relative ages of sands in the same desert.

In the Western Desert, Bagnold had made a lasting contribution to the understanding of arid terrain. He was among the first to analyze the wind's role in the movement of sand grains and in the formation of dunes.

"The free interplay of sand and wind has been allowed to continue undisturbed for a vast period of time, and here, if anywhere, it should be possible in the future to discover the laws of sand movement, and of growth of dunes," he theorized. Research based on his keen observations created the basis for present-day understanding of these laws. For his achievements, Bagnold was awarded the highly coveted Penrose Medal by the Geological Society of America, although he was a physicist, not a geologist.

The wind in the Sahara, as in most deserts, modifies everything in its path. It leaves its mark in many ways. Like a giant rake, the wind cuts deep parallel grooves into hard rock surfaces. These awesome striations mar rock outcrops for more than 60 miles in the open Sahara. Swirling with sand grains it has scooped up, the wind blasts irregular topography into eerie knobs. In the form of tiny whirling funnels, the wind polishes surfaces of hard rocks, such as chert. Like powerful drills it carves pits in the most solid rock. Rows of pits create fine flutes. These grooves form a surface texture similar to that of rocks photographed by the Viking landers on Mars. Could both the terrestrial and the Martian rocks have been pitted and fluted in the same way? Do Earth and Mars share a similar geological history? If so, some scientists believe it probable that tiny living plants could be thriving inside Martian rocks, just as blue-green algae live in the rocks found in the frigid desert climate of Antarctica.

"Your Farafra rocks are amazingly similar to those I just saw in Antarctica," geochemist Everett Gibson said to me after one of my lectures on landforms near Farafra Oasis. He opened his (Continued on page 26)

Cold light of the Arctic sun falls across the oil-rich North Slope, part of a polar desert in Alaska (opposite). A frozen region qualifies as a desert if it receives less than ten inches of precipitation annually. Below: In Antarctica—the world's southern polar desert—Taylor Valley bares a rocky terrain covered by a glacier as recently as 250,000 years ago.

GEORG GERSTER

NATIONAL GEOGRAPHIC PHOTOGRAPHER EMORY KRISTOF

*M*ajor dunes: In southern Africa's Namib Desert, seasonal, multidirectional winds fashion star dunes (right). Slight shifts in the prevailing wind create wriggling seif dunes in Egypt's Western Desert (bottom). In South America's Peruvian Desert, steady winds build crescent-shaped dunes called barchans (below).

LOREN MCINTYRE (TOP); GEORG GERSTER (ABOVE AND RIGHT)

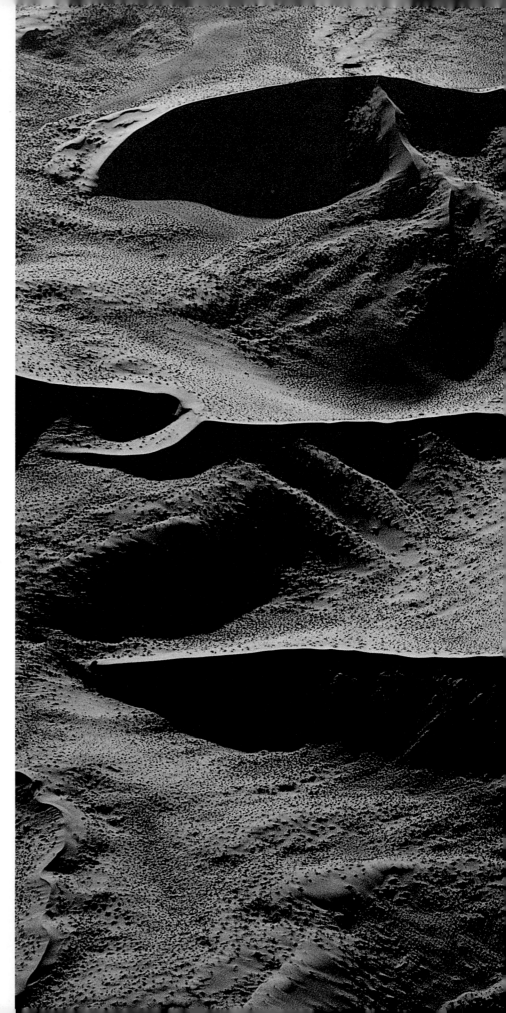

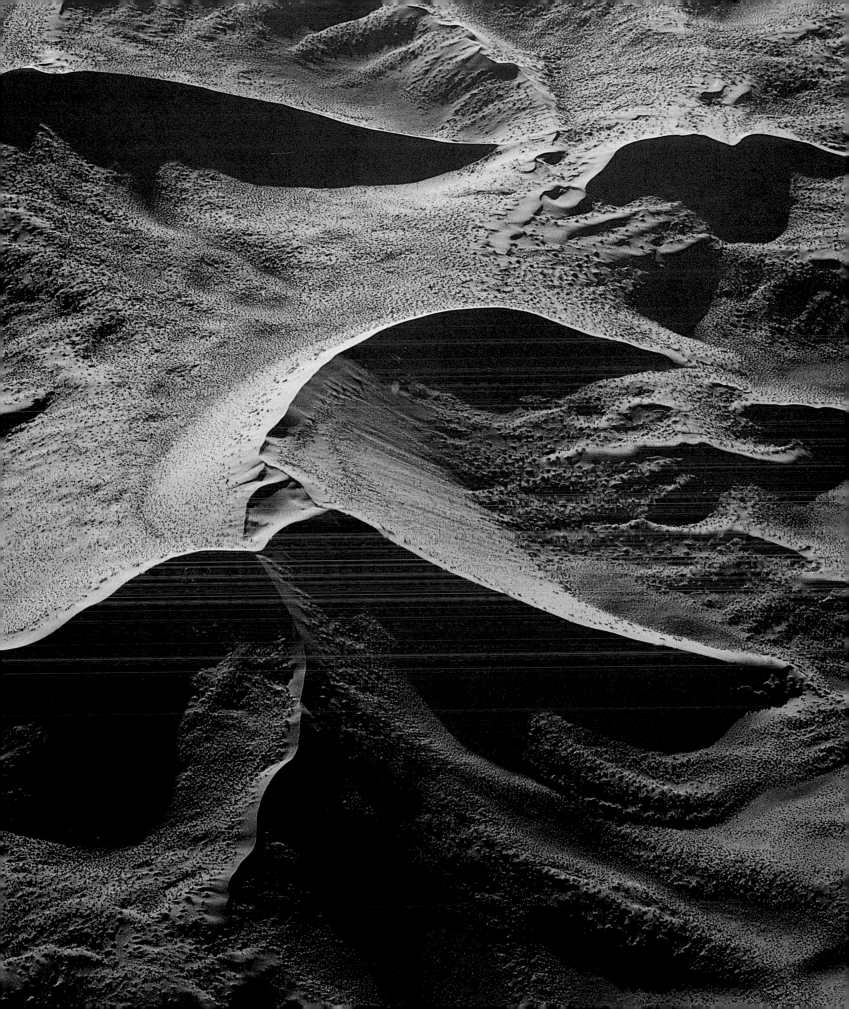

Streamlined by the wind, rock formations called yardangs lace the floor of the Namib Desert (below). In Egypt's Western Desert Dr. Farouk El-Baz, contributing author and consultant to The Desert Realm, *studies a rock outcrop (opposite). Empty mud nests of mason bees pepper the rock's leeward face. Fist-size rocks illustrate in miniature how lee dunes form (opposite, below).*

briefcase and pulled out photographs of one of Antarctica's dry valleys. He was right. The wind-eroded landforms from one of the hottest places on earth and those from one of the coldest regions looked remarkably similar. These wind-sculptured outcrops stand as silent witnesses to the power of wind.

Of all the wind's creations, yardangs are the most astounding. These finely chiseled rocks are more or less aerodynamically stable landforms that resemble inverted boat hulls. Some measure as long and as tall as a seagoing yacht. Fleets of yardangs, prows facing the wind and sterns pointing toward the lee, cover huge expanses in many deserts.

The desert wind is also a powerful agent of transportation. Its carrier system proceeds in measurable orderliness and depends on the capacity of air currents to sort out and segregate particles by grain size. The wind sifts out the finest exposed particles and hurls them into the atmosphere as dust.

Skylab astronauts observed the trail of a Saharan dust storm that blew from Africa's west coast across the Atlantic into the Caribbean. Air masses carry several hundred million tons of dust westward from the North African Sahara each year. This airborne veil, which occasionally drapes across the horizon, filters the sunlight and explains why sunsets on the east coast of Florida are sometimes golden yellow rather than the more common red.

The whirling force of desert storms also exposes large particles that resist the lifting power of the wind. Arranged as if by a master tile craftsman, these pebbles veneer a roadlike surface with a layer one grain thick. Stretches of this protective pavement are a desert driver's dream; vehicles speed across them with stability and ease at more than 60 miles an hour.

Some sand particles, those too large to be carried aloft and too small to defy the force of the wind, roll and bounce across the surface of the desert. On a gravel plain, like the Gobi in China and Mongolia, bouncing grains jump higher than they would on a sandy plain. Moving sand produces one of the most familiar features of the desert—dunes.

Accumulations of sand in the form of dunes can be simple, where the individuality of each dune is clear and separable; compound, where two or more dunes of the same kind merge by overlapping each other; or complex, where dunes of different shapes combine. Most distinctive are the crescent-shaped barchan dunes, the linear dunes, and the star dunes.

"I tell you, dunes are breathing creatures like other living creations of God!" remarked a young villager from Kharga Oasis in the Western Desert.

"Why do you say that?" I asked.

"Because dunes grow, they squeak and breed offspring of the same kind. Some dunes give birth to dunes of a different shape," he said.

I nodded. "We believe that the shape of a dune depends on the supply of sand and the velocity of the wind."

"All I know," said the villager, "is that the crescent dunes we are battling here in Kharga come from one big dune train north of us. Have you seen that?"

"Yes, I have." I unfolded my field notebook, took out a Landsat image and showed him the southern tip of Ghard Abu Muharik, a huge linear dune north of the young man's village. Ghard Abu Muharik is not one of a kind, either in the Western Desert or in other deserts. Enormous linear dunes occur as individual ridges, and several may group together and form a cluster of dunes. A large number of dunes make a sand sea. Some dune fields are stabilized by natural vegetation as in Australia and India but, in the Western Desert, dunes shift constantly with the wind. In the Kharga basin crescent dunes have engulfed whole villages.

"**B**ut dunes don't move, I know this for a fact!" This pronouncement startled me because it came from a surveyor and mapmaker.

"If dunes didn't move," I said, "they wouldn't have formed in the first place. We have just measured the rate of motion of crescent dunes in the Kharga basin. These dunes creep forward at a speed of 65 to 330 feet per year."

The surveyor shook his head. "I tracked a dune near a surveying camp and it didn't move much at all in seven years."

Bewildered, I asked, "Was it in a flat, open terrain?"

"No, it was enclosed in a valley."

"Did the wind there often change direction with the seasons?"

"Yes, quite a bit."

What the man had observed was a star dune, a formation with several extending arms that result from multidirectional winds. Such dunes are considered to be in perpetual motion, but always in the same spot, as if marching in place. Their steep faces rotate with each shift in the wind direction. In some areas the wind continues to pile the sand in enormous peaked heaps, forming pyramid dunes, such as those in the Taklimakan Desert of China.

"Is this a climbing or a falling dune?" The question was posed to me by Subrata Sinha, an environmental geologist with the Geological Survey of India at Jaipur, the Pink City of Rajasthan, a state in northwestern India. We had driven 40 miles from Jaipur to survey the puzzling dune that now faced us. It was unlike those in the Sahara. It boasted no sharp crests or steep faces, just an elongate mass of sand with gently sloping sides, like a great whale resting its head on a hill. Similar dunes covered the eastern, leeward flanks of the Aravalli Range. The sand had accumulated at some time in the past when the local climate was much drier. When rainfall increased, vegetation grew on the sand, holding it fast and concealing signs of the direction of dune buildup and motion —clues that could help us better understand the work of the wind ages ago. For these reasons, I could not answer my colleague's question. The landscape became less puzzling as we moved westward from Jaipur into the heart of Rajasthan. The land displayed a rolling topography of compound, U-shaped parabolic dunes in candelabra patterns with prongs pointing upwind. Most of the dunes were frozen in place by a cover of grasses, shrubs, and trees. In the far western parts of Rajasthan, near Pakistan, these parabolic dunes yield to linear and crescent dunes, all partly covered by vegetation.

Although some Middle Paleolithic artifacts were recently found in the Great Indian Desert in northern Rajasthan, continuous human habitation of this part of the world dates back only about 10,000 years. The reverse situation exists in the Sahara. Geological and archaeological evidence in northern Africa confirms that the region was much wetter and supported many human settlements more than 5,000 years ago. After that period the Sahara eventually dried up and most of it was forsaken by nearly all forms of life. In contrast, the Rajasthan must have been much drier about 10,000 *(Continued on page 30)*

GEORG GERSTER (ALL)

Desert derby: Under the whips of their riders, dromedaries lope neck and neck, reaching speeds up to 14 miles an hour in the King's Camel Race at Riyadh, capital of Saudi Arabia (opposite). Winners have received gold ceremonial daggers and cash purses worth more than $10,000. But the Saudis— descendants of ancient desert herders who bred the camel for endurance and speed—find the thrill and prestige of victory more exciting than the prizes. Binoculars bring the race closer to a spectator wearing the traditional red-and-white Saudi headdress (right). Enthusiasts atop water tankers strain for a better view (below). Motor vehicles have almost ended the camel's centuries-long reign as the chief means of transportation in the Arabian deserts. Most Bedouin who range the sands now do so in trucks. Many desert herdsmen, however, have walked away from the nomadic life to take urban jobs created by Saudi Arabia's petroleum industry.

ROBERT AZZI/WOODFIN CAMP & ASSOCIATES (ALL)

years ago, before the present wet phase introduced the stabilizing vegetation.

"Perhaps we must compare the Sahara with the Rajasthan to understand the natural changes in both," an archaeologist friend had suggested. An interesting prospect, that of comparing extremely arid northern Africa—one of the most desolate and uninhabited places on earth—with a region in northwest India—one of the world's most heavily populated arid lands. The suggestion has prompted the planning of a research project that holds promise of unearthing more knowledge of how climatic changes have affected not only landforms, but life itself.

The ability of living things to adapt in order to survive in dry climates is one of nature's most fascinating gifts. Today thousands of species of plants and animals and nearly a billion people, one-fifth of the world's population, live in semiarid, arid, and hyperarid lands.

"You look like a Christmas tree," I remember kidding one of my colleagues as he emerged from his desert tent, weighted down by elaborate field gear hanging from his shoulders, neck, and waist.

"I know!" he cried. "I envy you in your *galabia.*"

He was referring to my attire, a full-length robe that allows air to circulate about the body without the constriction of pants belted at the waist. The *kufieya*, a headdress, blocks the sun's rays and creates an air-conditioned environment about the head. This cool attire limits loss of body water and reduces drinking water requirements. Classic examples of adjustment to the environment, the robe and headdress have been worn by desert dwellers for centuries.

Every time I see photographs of World War II troops in North Africa, I pity the soldiers, who were burdened by field garb designed for cold and wet climates. Their uniforms constricted air movement at all conceivable points. Their berets inadequately covered their heads and left their necks open to the burning sun and their faces exposed to the persistent dust.

"Why don't we learn from local people?" lamented architect Hassan Fathy. Vigorous in his 80s, Fathy preaches the use of mud brick rather than concrete for desert buildings. During his long career he has meticulously studied the dome-shaped houses built by the Nubians before sections of their ancient land were flooded behind the High Dam at Aswan. The mud or clay brick used by the Nubians formed a more effective heat insulator and provided a building material less expensive than concrete. Their domed roofs with central vents allowed hot inside air to escape. Without the aid of artificial air conditioning, temperatures inside a Nubian-style house remained at least 20 degrees cooler than the outdoor temperatures.

Long before man learned to live with aridity, many plant forms had adapted to dryness and extreme temperatures in the world's deserts. The saguaro cactus, for example, can expand to store vast supplies of water. The physiological functions of many animals have also been altered. For instance, blood vessels in the long ears of the jackrabbit help regulate body temperature. Such features represent the success of selected traits perfected through generations of false starts and dead ends. Beginning on page 284, a special supplement to *The Desert Realm* highlights some of the *(Continued on page 39)*

Preserving old ways, an Omani elder wafts the fragrant smoke of frankincense to perfume his beard at the end of a meal (opposite). Most of the world's frankincense comes from the sap of Boswellia sacra *trees growing in Oman. People have burned the aromatic resin since biblical times to symbolize the sweet scent of heaven. They also have taken it as medicine, believing it a cure for ulcers and dysentery. Once a major export, frankincense now sells only locally. Oil income supports the economy of Oman.*

LYNN ABERCROMBIE

30

Winds fan an ancient passive cooling system in hot, dry central Iran. In a garden pavilion near the city of Yazd, a pool (opposite) humidifies air entering open doors and windows; outside, wind—speeding up as it flows over the domed roof—creates a partial vacuum that draws warm indoor air up and out through vents. Left: In a similar fashion, a domed cistern keeps water cool. Air flows down the inside of the flanking wind towers, called badgirs, and out through the vented dome, cooling the water by evaporation. Below: A hostess entertains guests beneath an outlet grille of a badgir in her home. Depending on time of day, temperature, and prevailing winds, air moving up or down in the tower produces cooling breezes at the outlet. Air cooled in the badgir at night makes mornings in the house the most refreshing time.

GEORG GERSTER (ALL)

PRECEDING PAGES: *High in the Andes of Chile, flamingos feed in Laguna Lejia on the Puna de Atacama. Dry desert air hastens evaporation, which increases mineral concentration in the area's brine-water lakes. Eventually, the lakes dry up, becoming snow-white salt flats called salars.*

F. GOHIER/PHOTO RESEARCHERS, INC. (PRECEDING PAGES)

*I*n pack-train formation, camels led by a horseman file through a nomad camp on the steppeland of the Mongolian People's Republic (left). The semiarid terrain supports a thin layer of drought-resistant grass. A Mongolian herder and his family may move 50 times a year in search of water and suitable pasture for their animals. To move family belongings, the nomads have traditionally used Bactrian camels (left)—the two-hump variety native to central Asia—and occasionally one-hump Arabian camels (above). Both animals grow shaggy coats for warmth in the cold Mongolian winters. The camels can travel for days without drinking and can carry large loads great distances on small amounts of food. Such endurance has made the beasts ideal work animals for people in arid lands. Above, opposite: A child of the steppe learns early to care for camels, sheep, and other herd animals, for they supply food, wool for clothing, and other essentials of life. Today many young Mongolians choose not to follow in the austere footsteps of their pastoral parents. The youngsters have their eyes on jobs in the city and on state-operated farms.

HOWARD SOCHUREK/WOODFIN CAMP & ASSOCIATES (LEFT); NATIONAL GEOGRAPHIC PHOTOGRAPHER GEORGE F. MOBLEY (ABOVE, OPPOSITE); GEORGE HOLTON/OCELOT (ABOVE)

37

adaptations of humans, animals, and plants to dry, hot climates. Features of the desert environment perceived as hostile by some people can be hospitable to those who have learned to live with aridity.

"Why is everyone so concerned about blown sand?" asked Eugene Sekaquaptewa of the Hopi Research and Development Company on the Hopi Reservation in northern Arizona. He had directed the question to our group, an international team of desert experts from as far away as China. We had gathered to study the arid lands of the United States. "Dunes in Egypt may be a curse, but here they are a blessing," he proclaimed.

"Why?" I asked.

"Without windblown sand we could not raise our crops. I will show you." He led us out into a field of sand surrounded by soil void of mulch and too hard to support any plants other than scraggly desert bushes. On the sand a Hopi farmer was digging a small pit. Into the hole he dropped kernels of blue corn. He walked a few paces and planted more seeds in the same way. He continued the process along straight lines, always keeping a distance between plantings to allow the seeds to feed on whatever water might accumulate. The sand absorbs meager precipitation like a sponge and protects the moisture in underlying soil from the evaporating rays of the sun.

In another field we observed the same process. This time the plants were surrounded by tin cylinders made from empty food cans. The metal protected the sprouting plants from the chafing wind and from grazing animals. Nearly all the planting was done in this manner, and with success. Peach orchards and other trees blossomed on the dunes.

One of the Chinese guests in our group looked at me and said, "What the Hopi have done here is something very Chinese."

"You mean that in China you farm like the Hopi?" I asked.

"No," he said, "I mean taking a bad thing and turning it into a good thing."

The destiny of desert lands is beginning to emerge in a new light as more people become familiar with these domains that have kindled feelings of fear on the one hand and feelings of romanticism on the other. An analogy involves a desert not of this world. Between 1967 and 1972, I helped select lunar sites for the landing missions and helped train astronauts in lunar geology and photography during the Apollo program. In those years I was often asked: "The moon used to be a romantic place associated with soft beauty. Now that you have seen its pockmarked surface strewn with rock rubble, haven't you lost your old feelings for it?"

"On the contrary," I would reply. "To me, as we learned more about the moon, it became a more friendly place. I began to see beauty that had been unknown to me—magnificent beauty that has filled my mind with lasting impressions." So it is with world deserts. The more I understand them, the less hostile and the more beautiful and inviting they appear. Worldwide, such enlightenment is slowly inspiring people to look toward the desert for the resources of fertile soil, underground water, and mineral wealth.

Clearly, the time has come for us to learn how to preserve the desert's beauty as we take some of the land and, in the words of my Chinese colleague, "turn it into a good thing."

STEPHEN J. KRASEMANN/DRK PHOTO (BELOW);
IAN BEAMES/ARDEA LONDON (OPPOSITE)

Creamy flower of a saguaro cactus peeks from a cluster of buds. The plants can bloom in the dry months of May and June because they have stored water from earlier spring rains, such as the shower in Arizona (opposite). The saguaros' ribbed trunks expand to hold moisture. Some of the largest plants contain as much as six tons of water. One 36-hour freeze could kill them; thus saguaros grow only in the hot Sonoran Desert of North America.

FOLLOWING PAGES: *"The Dragon," a 300-foot-high dune, commands the Pacific coast near Iquique in Chile. Southerly winds sweeping along the shore forged the dune's razorback shape.*

GEORG GERSTER (FOLLOWING PAGES)

39

GEORG GERSTER (BELOW); DR. J.A.L. COOKE/OXFORD SCIENTIFIC FILMS (FAR RIGHT)

Campfire cadence of clapping hands crackles with intricate Bushman rhythms (left). Among the world's last hunter-gatherers, the San— commonly called Bushmen—have roamed the Kalahari Desert in southern Africa for at least 20,000 years. The wanderers subsist mainly on moisture-laden plants in a land notorious for its scant surface water. Above: Like sea mist, sand blows from the crest of a dune in the Namib Desert. This hyperarid region runs 1,300 miles along the Atlantic coast of southern Africa. Ocean fog rolling inland brings moisture that sustains species of spiders, beetles, and reptiles found in no other corner of the world. The Namib's hardy flora and fauna attest to the ability of living things to survive by adapting to the rigors of the desert environment. Demands for change imposed by the 20th century endanger long-standing ways of life in many deserts. Nevertheless, lizards still skitter across dunes, plants still bloom in the face of aridity, and songs still fill the desert night.

Rocky Vistas and Wild Valleys

North America's Great Basin, Sonoran, Mojave, and Chihuahuan

By Tom Melham

West Texas winter: Ice-encrusted prickly pear cactus and foggy Chisos Mountains give a wet look to Big Bend National Park, part of the Chihuahuan Desert. Twelve to fifteen inches of rain a year can fall in North America's dry regions, making them some of the wettest and greenest deserts in the world.

© DAVID MUENCH 1982

44

We are water creatures, you and I, born not of deserts but of the sea. Salt water bathes our eyes, cools our skin, gives form to each cell. It enables muscles to move and minds to dream. It is part of our lifeblood, our very selves.

So to us the desert seems alien, incomplete, a savage mix of earth, air, and fiery sun totally lacking that fourth and most human element, water.

Enter dry Death Valley in summertime, when ground temperatures edge toward 200°F and your water-loving, 98°F self feels as perishable as a lettuce leaf. Or spend an especially hot August day in southern Arizona's desert, watching dust devils funnel across this broad, dry land of big sun and little shade. The air—incredibly transparent and light at dawn—becomes heavy by midday. Hour by hour the stranglehold tightens. Stay too long and lungs gasp; legs bog down. Horizons belly dance to ever rising heat waves.

But suddenly, a hint of reprieve: Stagnant air begins to churn; thunderheads materialize and blunder forth in a darkening armada. Tall and silent as square-riggers, they run before now-gusting winds, dumping cargoes of rain, then rapidly sail off.

And so, in its season, water comes to the desert. Arroyos that hold not a drop most of the year can rage with torrents several feet deep. Such flash floods occur throughout much of North America's deserts, where hard-packed soil and heavy, localized cloudbursts dictate rapid runoff. Flat washes may seem like ideal campsites, but beware. Rainfall so distant that you don't see it could drain your way, arriving without warning in a scouring wall of water that instantly erases almost all life, then quietly melts into the sand. Every year more people *drown* in North America's arid regions than die there from lack of water.

This unfortunate fact underlines a simple truth about North American deserts: They rank among the wettest and greenest in the world. On rare occasions, certain areas have received more than 20 inches of rain in a year, more than ten times the average for the Sahara. Some of the arid regions, like many world deserts, lie atop vast aquifers of groundwater, while others flank major rivers such as the Rio Grande, the Colorado, and their tributaries. In short, water is as basic to many of the continent's deserts as sunshine. Much less plentiful, of course, but abundant enough to generate a wealth of unusual plants. The resultant greenery has baffled many a foreign visitor. Eyes familiar with barren sand wastes of North Africa do not easily recognize North America's shrub-, cactus-, and yucca-spotted wilderness as genuine desert.

But desert it is, often split along botanical lines into the Big Four—the Great Basin, Mojave, Sonoran, and Chihuahuan Deserts. Sagebrush, shadscale, and other shrubs dominate the Great Basin, North America's coldest and largest desert; it spans almost all of Nevada and most of Utah, as well as portions of six other states. The Joshua tree—an especially large and many-branched species of yucca—helps define the dry and generally low-lying Mojave, home of Death Valley. Saguaro cactuses taller than telephone poles brand the Sonoran Desert, which boasts the desert world's greatest variety of plants. Dagger-leaved agaves and yuccas catch storm-blown moisture from the Gulf of Mexico and brighten the Chihuahuan Desert, a vast plateau rising as high as 6,000 feet between opposite flanks of the Sierra Madre Oriental and the Sierra Madre Occidental ranges in Mexico.

From the Pacific Northwest to central Mexico, North America's arid lands blanket 730,000 square miles. With valleys below sea level and mountains a mile high, the region breaks into the Big Four: the Great Basin, Mojave, Sonoran, and Chihuahuan Deserts. Most experts have defined these areas loosely rather than with exact geographical borders. The Great Basin, largest of the four, takes in portions of eight western states from the Sierra Nevada to the Rockies. The Mojave, the smallest, slopes eastward from the Sierra Nevada in southern California to the Colorado River and runs north into Nevada. The Sonoran, the most botanically varied, straddles the Gulf of California. The Chihuahuan, the most isolated, covers a triangular plateau between the Sierra Madre Occidental and the Sierra Madre Oriental in Mexico and extends into Texas and New Mexico.

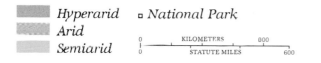

Hyperarid	▫ National Park
Arid	
Semiarid	

KILOMETERS
0 — 000
STATUTE MILES
0 — 600

And what of the Painted Desert? Colorado Desert? Mexico's El Gran Desierto, and dozens more? These are smaller, local deserts, often so poorly defined that their borders and even their names vary from map to map. To avoid confusion—and to underscore similarities—most scientists usually consolidate them in the four major sections that together total approximately 730,000 square miles.

But names and subdivisions make up only a minor part of the Big Four's whole story. Look at the *land.* Drink in its lonesomeness, its gorgeous desolation. Bare rock and sand, studded here and there with spartan desert plants. It is all so skeletal. No leafy forests flesh out these bones or obscure the view. Your eyes wander over windblown dunes, perhaps, or seemingly endless rolling plateaus, black lava fields, corrugated salt flats, or down river-sculpted canyons unlike any other in the world. Timeless, broad, alluring—yet achingly empty—this landscape is built on a scale so sweeping and stark that it tugs instantly at your emotions.

Some of the region's thick-skinned plants can seem almost alien. Scatterings of leathery cactuses and scraggly shrubs, prickly arrays of thorns, sharp spines, and stiletto leaves tend to keep humans at a distance.

Desert creatures can have the same effect. Rattlesnakes and scorpions, vultures and bats, hairy tarantulas as big as a hand, stink beetles that stand on their heads, lizards that squirt blood through their eyes—these and other varmints repel more often than they attract. Such elaborate behavior enables the animals to survive in a land of scarcity.

Even the land of the North American deserts can seem strange. Reality and fantasy merge. Clouds seem carved out of granite, and solid rock billows up in

Tapping the desert's greatest resource, a 33-unit housing development (above) hooks up to solar power in the Los Angeles area, which appears turquoise against the black Pacific Ocean in a Landsat image (opposite). The yellow-fringed triangle contains the Mojave Desert, bounded by the San Andreas Fault on the southwest and the Garlock Fault on the northwest. Red rectangles indicate irrigated farmland.

FOLLOWING PAGES: *Tracking mirrors focus sunlight on a solar tower at an experimental plant designed to provide electric power for southern California.*

NATIONAL GEOGRAPHIC PHOTOGRAPHER
JAMES L. STANFIELD
(ABOVE AND FOLLOWING PAGES)

fluffy mounds. It's a fierce, hard land ruled by mirage and mystery, by mare's-tail clouds and slickrock sculptures and limbless trees of stone. A land of colossal proportions, not city-bred closenesses. Of peyote eaters and, yes, magic. Indians who live here know this—the Pima, Papago, Apache, Paiute, Yaqui, Navajo, Hopi, and many other tribes. Animists all, each believes that certain natural forms, such as water, clouds, plants, a tumbling rock, possess conscious life and power.

Hard to believe? Pause a moment beside Racetrack, and see if you can offer a better explanation for its mysterious *moving rocks.* Racetrack is a playa, or evaporated lake—a virtually flat, 2½-mile-long oval of dried mud locked between two ridges of the Panamint Range in Death Valley National Monument, part of the Mojave Desert, the smallest and driest of the Big Four. The name "Racetrack" may stem from early prospectors' tales that Indians raced horses here. Hardly anything grows on these flats. But they are not totally empty. At the northern end of the playa stand two bedrock islands, the larger one a low, craggy outcrop called The Grandstand. Widely scattered rocks ranging from mere pebbles to boulders that weigh as much as 700 pounds dot the playa's otherwise vacant surface.

Strangely, many have left tracks. Shallow ruts, sometimes no more than one-eighth of an inch deep but wandering on for hundreds of feet, etch Racetrack's concrete-hard mud, occasionally angling back on themselves. You follow a trail, and it usually ends at a rock. Few other marks gouge the playa's smooth skin, so no one could have dragged these stones into place. They appear to have traveled all by themselves, as if nature had turned loose some battery-powered toys and then had forgotten to recharge them.

At least eight other playas in this part of the desert boast similarly mobile rocks. Although no one has ever seen them slide about, periodic measurements prove that they do just that.

But how?

Most geologists credit some combination of wind and rain. The playa's fine clay becomes extremely slick when wet, they note, and occasional gales rip through the valley, most often in winter. If just the right amount of rain falls—too much would bog down the rocks—high winds could power Racetrack's wandering stones, geologists theorize. Ice could also play a role.

It's hard to accept that boulders move at the whim of mere wind. It can gust to high speeds, however, when funneled through a narrow mountain gap at the southwest end of the playa. Still the movement of each stone involves a set of conditions so complex that they're not easily explained by scientists. But an old man of Indian ancestry I met in one of the dustier corners of the Mojave had a simple solution.

"The rocks move," Jake told me, "because they can."

An admirable statement. One that wastes no words, and one that echoes the mood of the desert. To Jake, as to Indians past, wondering how rocks move is as senseless as pondering how rabbits run or how water falls or how earth exists. What many city people see as oddities of nature—the salt sculptures of Death Valley, for example—are not odd at all, but only normal. *We* are the strange ones. *(Continued on page 52)*

Dune buggies, motor homes, jeeps, and other ORVs—off-road vehicles—converge on California's El Mirage lake bed (left). Near Death Valley (opposite), a dune buggy challenges the crests of the Dumont Sand Dunes. Many drivers, reveling in the unpaved freedom of the Mojave Desert, admit that their hobby gouges a terrain that easily erodes. Ecologists worry about North America's fragile deserts. They say the land's thin skin of protective plants can take years to recover—if it ever does—from the ravages of a single day of ORV fun.

One summer I weathered a storm on Racetrack. Winds blew and rain fell—but not a pebble moved, at least none I had marked. I left as sunbeams slowly returned, backlighting the still falling rain and igniting a double rainbow over the playa. On my way down the rock-strewn trail I was surprised to see a silhouette waving to me from the ridge high above—a lone backpacker in this wilderness, up to catch the sun's last rays. About a half-mile farther on, I caught sight of *another* backpacker, also beckoning. Then a third and a fourth. Only then did I realize that my "hikers" were really windblown Joshua trees.

Up close, this wildly branched plant sheathed in bayonet leaves suggests a gangly and many-armed porcupine more than it does a person. But distance and desert light foster a milder image. Each lone silhouette on that mountain looked as human as its name—bestowed more than a century ago by Mormon pioneers who associated its eerie presence with the Biblical prophet, beckoning them toward their Promised Land.

Built more of pith than of wood, Joshua trees belong to the lily family. They are yuccas—lilies adapted to arid conditions, just as thorny mesquites and palo verde trees are transformed pea plants, and just as the cactus is the desert relative of the rose. Newcomers to the desert often assume that cactuses dominate all the world's arid regions. They do not. They are native only to the Western Hemisphere, and though they range from Canada to Argentina, rarely do they abound. The Great Basin, for example, harbors very few cactus species despite its size.

NATIONAL GEOGRAPHIC PHOTOGRAPHER BRUCE DALE (BOTH)

Cactuses like it hot, growing mainly in the Sonoran Desert, a 120,000-square-mile horseshoe that rims the Gulf of California. Some 300 types of cactuses, ranging from mushroom-size peyote to Mexico's 70-foot-high cardon, thrive here. Often they bear delightfully fitting common names. Barrel Cactus. Prickly Pear. Fishhook. Organ Pipe. Hedgehog. Rainbow. Candelabra. Old Man.

Then there is Hollywood's favorite unsalaried extra—the saguaro featured in countless western movies. This humanoid-shaped plant with upraised arms and waist-thick body has come to symbolize the entire Southwest. In reality, however, the saguaro is native only to the Sonoran Desert, where it prefers the sunny southern sides of hills.

Saguaros are the desert's water towers. Each plant's shallow but wide-ranging roots efficiently suck whatever moisture soaks into the gravelly soil and pass it on to an accordion-pleated trunk, which expands and contracts as needed. The trunk stores enough water so that the saguaro not only survives droughts but also comes to fruit during the driest time of year, May and June. Desert Indians, such as the Papago of southern Arizona, revere this cactus. Its sweet fruit once fed them through the empty time of year and was a harbinger of summer rains that revived both wild and domesticated plants critical to their diet. The Papago calendar—based on changes in the land rather than in solar positions—begins with phases in the saguaro cycle. Each new year's cactus harvest, followed by the making of saguaro wine, has always been a most important event to them. For Juanita Ahil it still is. (Continued on page 59)

JEN & DES BARTLETT/BRUCE COLEMAN LTD. (LEFT); PETER L. KRESAN (BELOW AND BOTTOM, LEFT)

*C*actus and rock rule the Sonoran Desert's Pinacate region in Mexico (right). Tufts cap a boojum tree, a rare species native only to a few areas in Mexico (above). In Baja California, turkey buzzards perch like living totems on cardon cactuses (top).

Death Valley, hottest, driest, and lowest region in North America: Craggy salt deposits corrugate the Devil's Golf Course (left), formed when salty groundwater surfaced and vaporized in the sun. Ground temperatures as high as 190°F bake Death Valley's warped terrain, which dips 282 feet below sea level. Below: A dry lake bed called Racetrack has mystified visitors for generations with moving rocks that leave shallow trails in the parched clay. Geologists believe that high winds propel these stones, some of which weigh several hundred pounds, when rainstorms turn Racetrack's hard surface into slippery mud. Right: Death Valley's gully-scarred hills, gravel washes, and flood-felled trees betray the occasional yet powerful presence of water in the Mojave Desert.

JIM BRANDENBURG/BRUCE COLEMAN INC.

PAUL CHESLEY (BELOW AND LEFT)

Sunrise in late June—and already Juanita is up, seeing to the fires in her saguaro camp. Furnishings for the month-long harvest are modest: a cot, some food bins and cookpots and clothes, a water barrel, a chair or two, a crude ramada to shield her from the devastatingly direct sunlight. There is nothing else, apart from a cooler of Coors.

Less than five feet tall and more than 75 years old, Juanita stoops slightly as her deeply furrowed, acorn-brown face methodically scans the horizon for the best path to the most saguaros. She sucks thoughtfully on a beer, chases it with a quick dipperful of water, and is off. One hand carries an empty lard pail, the other her *kuipad*—the traditional harvesting stick some 15 feet long, made of woody saguaro ribs lashed together.

I follow, hustling to keep up with a pace still fast and steady despite her years. Dodging the bur sage, cholla, and prickly pear that spot the Sonoran landscape, we soon come to a saguaro whose green, plum-size fruits wear the pink blush of proper ripeness. Dull green, she explains, means unripe; dark red is overripe, a burst fruit.

Up goes the kuipad. Deftly Juanita flicks off the desired fruits—they do not ripen all at once—and then bends low to gather them. Still attached to each are the dried remains of the cactus's flower, surprisingly hard and sharp. Juanita snaps off one of these knifelike floral tubes and uses it to slit the fruit's thick rind. There is an instant explosion of color as she everts the drab husk, revealing its deep, voluptuously red pulp, peppered with black, poppylike seeds. The red is so luscious it seems dangerous to eat—artificial almost, far more brilliant than strawberry or watermelon.

Into her lard pail goes the plucked fruit, and Juanita moves on, filling the bucket in about two hours. She wastes little time, for already the air is heating up, and she must compete with the birds, rodents, insects, and other animals that also relish the saguaro's once-a-year gift.

Back in camp, she boils the harvest over glowing mesquite logs, adding only a few quarts of water and a lot of heat. I help myself to a mouthful of pulp and find it sweet but disappointingly bland, a faint strawberry taste punctuated by the crunch of hundreds of tiny seeds. The pulp and seeds—rich in edible oils—Juanita will strain out and set aside to dry. Later they can be made into any of 11 food products, including jam, ground flour, or simply roasted seeds to be mixed with sugar and eaten as a snack. The filtered red liquid returns to the fire, cooking down after several hours into a thick, dark syrup. It's a traditional Papago food, as is saguaro wine.

Juanita enthusiastically shares her wine recipe: She takes equal parts of syrup and water, mixes them, and lets them ferment for two days in the hot sun. If left any longer, the wine will sour, she warns. For this reason, and because the tribe believes that the more one saturates oneself with the wine, the more the ground will be saturated later with rain, old-time Papago consumed their entire vintage in a day or two.

This custom is only one of many examples of the boom-and-bust cycle basic to North America's deserts, where survival often has meant diets of wretched excess and even more wretched want. Although certain desert tribes dry-farmed corn, beans, and squash, they all (Continued on page 65)

Navajo Tinker Yazzie leads his horse down Arizona's Canyon de Chelly (opposite). Late arrivals to the Southwest, the Navajo learned from neighbors: Pueblo Indians taught them horsemanship and sheepherding. These skills became the bases for the Navajo's pastoral life. Settled Hopis showed the newcomers how to farm and to weave. Hopi cornfields still ripen in desert washes (below).

TERRY E. EILER (BOTH)

59

TERRY E. EILER (BOTH)

Dry-farming, a Hopi on an arid Arizona mesa depends on special corn varieties and careful timing rather than on irrigation. Just after spring rains, seeds go into the ground, where fast-growing roots push down to moist subsoil that will sustain the corn through dry months. Summer rains see the crop through to harvest (below). Hopi ancestors advanced dry-farming techniques in North America by building irrigation ditches, terraces, and small dams to retard soil erosion and to make the most of scarce moisture.

*W*ide, *wild world of contrast: Utah features The Needles (right)—red-rock sculptures in Canyonlands National Park—and the dead-level Bonneville Salt Flats (below). Buckled by geologic faulting, basins and mountain ranges seesaw across the dry landscape of Nevada (bottom).*

CRAIG SHERBURNE/WEST STOCK

© DAVID MUENCH 1982

SAM ABELL/WOODFIN CAMP & ASSOCIATES

depended at least somewhat on wild foods, alternately gorging themselves on whatever was in season and then going without.

They ate not only cactus fruits but also the desert's lizards and caterpillars and spinachy greens. Tender tips of cholla cactus were rolled in the sand to strip away spines, then roasted or boiled. Century plants—large agaves that take years to bloom—produced a starchy heart that could be roasted like a potato. The Indians roasted the agave hearts for two days to cook out natural toxic chemicals in the plants. Modern distillers use agaves to make Mexico's memorable tequila and mescal. Many other desert plants could help avert a worldwide food crisis predicted by some scientists for the turn of the century.

Dr. Richard S. Felger of the Arizona-Sonora Desert Museum near Tucson contends that conventional agriculture—despite all its advances—simply won't be able to cope with the problems of man's ever ballooning population and ever shrinking farmland. Erosion, desertification, salinization, and increasing urban sprawl continually deplete the earth's farmable soils. Although irrigation has made some deserts bloom, it is expensive, sometimes impractical, and it can permanently ruin the land.

One of the problems is that in arid regions evaporation so concentrates the salts dissolved in irrigation water that they eventually poison the soil. Hundreds of thousands of acres of once-irrigated western farms already have been abandoned, and some scientists now warn that California's lush Imperial Valley—carved from the desert—could in the future become too salty for any crop. Improved drainage might save the fields, but there may not be enough water or money to do the job. Ironically, the Imperial Valley sits atop an enormous geothermal aquifer, which contains great quantities of salty water that could possibly provide a solution to the problem. Water temperatures in the huge underground pool go as high as 572°F. Researchers are developing methods to use the steaming brine to generate electric power. They believe it's feasible that the clean waste water produced by a power plant could be used to dilute the salty water in the fields.

Meanwhile, current water-use practices continue to be controversial. For example, the multibillion-dollar Central Arizona Project will, when finished, divert Colorado River water to Phoenix and Tucson for industrial and urban use. It promises to reduce the cities' reliance on groundwater, currently being used faster than it can be replaced. But environmentalists believe that tapping the river is a short-term solution at best. In the long run, they say, the Colorado River—already overcommitted—will not be able to meet the increasing water demands of growing cities and farms.

Felger suggests an alternative: Rather than keep trying to alter desert *lands* to suit water-loving crops, why not adapt desert *plants* to our needs?

"There are 30,000 species of edible plants in the world," he says, "and we eat only about 3,000. We're ignoring the bulk of our most important resource—food." Domestication of the desert's naturally drought- and salt-resistant species, he emphasizes, would enable us to transform millions of square miles of "wasteland" into productive farms—without the problems of irrigation.

Dr. Heriberto Parra Hake, regional director of Mexico's National Institute for Forestry Research, agrees: "It's amazing that in all the centuries of civilization, man has used just five main grains—wheat, *(Continued on page 68)*

Springtime splash of California poppies gilds Arizona's Ajo Range (opposite) and contradicts the desert's reputation for drabness. North America's arid tracts support some of the desert world's hardiest shrubs, such as the yucca (bottom). The lands also provide a home for an array of insects, rodents, birds, and reptiles—such as the Gila monster (below).

ENTHEOS/STEVEN C. WILSON

ROBERT P. CARR/BRUCE COLEMAN LTD.
AND © DAVID MUENCH 1982 (OPPOSITE)

65

PETER L. KRESAN (ABOVE); TAD NICHOLS (RIGHT)

*D*aybreak highlights wisps of fog carrying scant moisture to a saguaro-studded slope in southern Arizona. Summer rains in this region of the Sonoran Desert often come in the form of thunderstorms. Downpours running off the hardpan soil can spawn flash floods (opposite). Mesquite, blue palo verde, and ironwood trees anchor close to arroyos, where runoff keeps the subsoil moist.

NATIONAL GEOGRAPHIC PHOTOGRAPHER
JAMES L. STANFIELD (BOTH)

corn, rice, barley, soy and other beans—out of all the world's plants. A sixth or seventh could be hiding in the desert; we've never really looked."

A strong candidate, both men feel, is mesquite: one of the thorny reasons why cowboys wear chaps.

"It's the most promising desert plant for the near future," says Felger, noting its wide distribution through all four North American deserts. "It grows quickly, producing maybe 20,000 pods per tree—yields sufficient for modern agricultural techniques. Because it occurs in several dozen varieties, it can be hybridized for the most desirable characteristics. Best of all, it's high in protein." Mesquite was a staple of many Indian tribes—until the white man's tastier, more convenient foods came along. But to those who criticize this desert bean as less than palatable, Felger counters: "If taste were a major concern, we never would have cultivated soybeans. Ten years ago, no one had ever heard of them except as cattle feed. Now they're everywhere. Soy protein was the miracle food of the seventies."

Does this mean Western-style fast-food chains will soon be serving mesquite burgers, along with agave fries and prickly pear milkshakes? Not yet, pardner. But stranger things have happened. After all, the milkshakes most places serve today are thickened with a seaweed derivative. Pop a Dynamint into your mouth, and you're reaping the fruit—actually the wax—of candelilla, a plant found in the Chihuahuan Desert.

Even if a new food isn't immediately forthcoming from the desert, a new cash crop probably is, says botanist Parra Hake. His research, based in the Sonoran Desert's beautifully forlorn Baja California, centers on jojoba, a shrub that has raised hopes of making desert farmers rich—and of saving sperm whales from extinction. Jojoba-seed oil, actually a liquid wax already used in some shampoos and soaps, has properties almost identical to those of sperm-whale oil needed for high-speed machinery. Jojoba oil so excites Parra Hake that he has turned playwright, authoring *La Jojoba y la Ballena*—The Jojoba and the Whale—"to educate people that desert plants are worthwhile."

The play's characters? Jojoba Seed, Whale, Mother Nature, Humanity—all wearing lifesize Muppetlike costumes. The plot? "Nature tells Humanity about things it has made," explains Parra Hake. "It asks, 'Why kill whales when you have other sources for what you kill them for? Don't you know about jojoba?'" Enter Jojoba Seed. He delivers a whale-saving soliloquy that eventually convinces Humanity to change its ways; both audience and characters exit happily.

The world, however, does not change so easily. Although human ideals and emotions may favor a quick end to whaling, hard economics do not. Today jojoba is simply too expensive and in too short supply to offer an immediate alternative. Recent market fluctuations have driven jojoba oil to an incredible $300 a gallon. Prices could drop once the plant is domesticated, but this and other genetic experimentation may not be perfected for jojoba in time to save many whales. While basic research is under way worldwide, such as selecting and hybridizing high-yield, disease-resistant varieties and devising technology to collect and propagate seeds, much remains to be done.

The same is true for other potential desert crops, such as a gray-green shrub called guayule. Native to the Chihuahuan Desert, guayule produces a latex very similar to that of tropical rubber trees. Wild guayule generated a tenth of the world's natural rubber in 1910. In World War II, the United States worked to develop guayule commercially, but the use of synthetic rubber made from petroleum sidelined the project. Today new squeezes on worldwide oil reserves have rekindled emphasis on the development of guayule in the U.S.

Dr. Jimmy Tipton, a research horticulturalist at Texas A&M University's Research and Extension Center at El Paso, expects tire companies to turn to guayule eventually. "Of course, you may never know it," he says. "Goodyear won't advertise them as guayule tires."

In the years ahead even the desert's most common plants might prove valuable for their biomass—the amount of organic matter in any particular area—renewable and readily convertible to alcohol, methane, and other clean-burning fuels. A potential biomass garden might be the Great Basin, for its 210,000 square miles define not only North America's largest desert but also the continent's least botanically varied dry region. Valleys of sagebrush cover much of its Nevada heartland, alternating almost endlessly with finger-like, parallel mountain ridges in a washboard monotony known as basin and range. You cross one parched basin and struggle up the bordering range eager for new vistas—only to find more of the same: a tawny flatland rimmed by more distant ridges and dotted with more sage.

Leave the Great Basin and you discover a dramatic change—the startlingly varied realm of the Colorado Plateau, which forms parts of Utah, Colorado, Arizona, and New Mexico. In front of you stretch approximately 150,000 square miles of canyons and pinnacles and mesas, of stone arches and colorfully striped palisades, of gorges both wet and dry. This is red-rock country. Most of it is appropriately red—although cliffs also wear various shades of green, yellow, blue, magenta, and lavender that blush and fade with the sun's daily movement. There is enough natural beauty here to support the densest concentration of national parks and monuments in the United States. Arches. Canyonlands. Dinosaur. Zion. Petrified Forest. The Grand Canyon. And on and on, totaling 27 separate areas under National Park Service supervision.

Except at high elevations where rain is more likely, the Colorado Plateau contains both semiarid and arid tracts. Viewed from a mesa top, the plateau can seem flat as a Nevada basin. But try to cross it and you run up against a riverine maze of chasms chopping the land into so many planes that your intended two-hour ramble turns into a three-day trek. Don't forget a canteen, for unless you stay close to one of the area's few rivers, water is strictly cache-or-carry.

This is rugged country—tough enough to have staved off explorers and settlers long after other frontiers had been tamed. Each canyon branches into numerous side canyons that in turn split into ever smaller gorges, creating millions of hideaways. No wonder the Navajo Indians made their last stand against Kit Carson here; no wonder outlaw bands hid so successfully here, prolonging the West's wildness into the 20th century.

It may seem a contradiction, but water built these dry landscapes, first laying down sediments that would become the colorful sandstones and limestones and shales, then sculpting and polishing these rocks as geologic pressures slowly uplifted the entire Plateau. *(Continued on page 72)*

Heart of controversy: Havasu Lake pumping station (above) promises, when finished, to push water from the Colorado River to Phoenix and Tucson through giant conduits and canals (opposite). Proponents of the Central Arizona Project aim to reduce groundwater use. Opponents think the project threatens the Colorado River, already overtaxed by water demands.

NATIONAL GEOGRAPHIC PHOTOGRAPHER JAMES L. STANFIELD

*C*oaxing the desert into bloom, irrigation sprinklers dole out Colorado River water to California's fertile Imperial Valley, the nation's salad bowl. Heavy reliance on irrigation can exact a high cost: Mineral salts accumulate in the waterlogged ground until crops can no longer grow. Such increasing salinization of the land, along with the steadily rising price of water in the arid West, has forced some farmers to turn their once-bountiful fields back to the desert.

Walk up Elephant Canyon, a twisting channel of water-polished slickrock in Canyonlands National Park. Its rocky walls are like glacial ice about to melt; all seems ready to move. Much already has. Overhangs weathered by wind and water and heaps of fallen stone attest to erosion's triumph over rock. Abruptly you come to Druid Arch—a massive, angular rock of ages, creating new fantasy shapes from its own decay. Once it was a solid knob; now two slits pierce this double arch, doomed to collapse eventually.

But today it stands rigid enough, backed by distant, snowcapped peaks that rise like a mirage above the simmering red rock of Elephant Canyon. Here, in summertime, snow has to be a lie—but it isn't. And yet there *is* an illusion, one stemming more from human prejudice than from desert heat. For too long, we water creatures have judged deserts as hot, dry, barren, useless. They have been wastelands, known not for their unique charms but for their lack of conventional appeal. First we avoided them, then we sought

Big Surf, a 2½-acre artificial lake (right) near Phoenix, uses city water to generate five-foot waves for surfing. The recreational facility loses 10,000 gallons of water a day to evaporation in Arizona's desert climate. In booming Sunbelt areas, debates over urban development surge. Critics say that growth endangers diminishing water supplies and threatens small agricultural operations (below).

FOLLOWING PAGES: *Drained to the point of exhaustion by cities and farms upstream, the Colorado River dies two miles from the Gulf of California.*

H. EDWARD KIM, NATIONAL GEOGRAPHIC STAFF (BOTH); NATIONAL GEOGRAPHIC PHOTOGRAPHER JAMES L. STANFIELD (FOLLOWING PAGES)

to conquer them. Perhaps now it's time to appreciate North America's deserts for what they *are*—and stop judging them in terms of what they are *not*.

What can they offer us water creatures, apart from a lot of rocks and strange plant life? Nothing, really. Nothing but the freedom that comes with walking the Colorado Plateau for a week and not seeing another human being. Nothing but the sudden realization that your footprints are marching side by side with the fossilized tracks of a lizard that scrambled over this very spot 50 million years ago. Nothing but thumbnail-size potsherds littering the ground, looking as new and plentiful as yesterday's ticker tape—but dating back centuries to the Anasazi, ancestors of many of today's Southwestern Indians. Nothing but raw beauty in a land apart, where time wears heavy yet centuries rush by. Where change comes every day and not at all. Where you can go when you are too full of civilization's clutter, too choked by the busy details of life. Here is a place where *nothing* can mean everything.

A place we need in order to survive.

Ocean Breezes and the Rain Shadow

Along South America's West Coast

Text and Photographs
by Loren McIntyre

Like splashes across an artist's palette, the algae-tinted waters of Laguna Colorada streak an arid playa high in Bolivia. South America's deserts— among the driest in the world —extend from the towering reaches of the Andean summits to the curving lowlands of fog-draped coasts.

Like Francisco Pizarro, who discovered this land in his search for the Inca Empire, I first sighted the Pacific coast of South America from a vessel out of Panama. The coastline stretched jungle green off the port bow of the freighter *Santa Maria.* Mangroves entangled the shore. I saw no hint of the fabulous desert beaches where that 16th-century Spaniard and his conquistadors had galloped south in quest of gold and glory.

On the morning of the fourth day, precisely when we rounded the westernmost cape of the continent, 275 nautical miles south of the Equator, the landscape turned to barren rock and sand, and the tropic air turned chill. We pitched through sleek swells. Porpoises closed on us like torpedoes, then swerved to parallel our course and leap our bow wave. Not far off, sperm whales spouted. Vast schools of little fish surfaced and shattered the warped mirror of the sea. Flights of boobies filled the sky, then emptied it all at once—diving like spent arrows into patches of fish-flung spume. We knifed through rafts of cormorants bending to the swells, dark acres of birds gulping frenzied fish. Sea lions lifted bewhiskered faces and watched our steel flanks slide by.

At my elbow, *Santa Maria*'s Chief Officer George Didriksen spoke of the north-flowing Peru Current. It had slowed our speed a knot or so. The Humboldt Current, he called it, after the scientist who first found it to be much colder than he expected for these tropical latitudes.

"It flows from the south," said Didriksen. "Subsurface water wells up against the continent, and all along the beaches it gives bathers goose pimples, although most of the beaches are closer to the Equator than Rio de Janeiro is." He described the water as some of the richest in the world. A single quart may teem with 40,000 microscopic plants and animals—called plankton. "The Peru Current helps create the desert," Didriksen added. "It inhibits rainfall by cooling and trapping moist air at the surface." He was referring to the temperature inversion—a layer of warm air over a layer of cold air—that fosters humidity higher than 80 percent, causing fog instead of rain.

Another reason for the desert's aridity is that the Andes block prevailing easterlies from the Amazon Basin. Mountains force wet air up to 20,000 feet. Chilled, it condenses and dumps as much as 120 inches of rain annually on the east slopes of the Andes, producing one of earth's densest rain forests. On the leeside, where little moisture falls, dry land slopes to the Pacific coast.

Close to shore, the soft wind wafted an odor of ammonia. The chief officer explained it was the smell of seabird excrement—guano—which accumulates on the more than 40 island rookeries along the coast. After a last long night, the *Santa Maria* docked in Callao, the seaport of Lima, capital of Peru. In that year—1947—Lima numbered 800,000 persons. Today earth-circling satellites see the city as a 17-mile-wide splotch of five million inhabitants—nearly half of all the people who dwell on the west-coast desert of South America.

The desert reaches roughly from latitude 5° South to 30° South, from the border of Ecuador to central Chile. The southern slice of this area includes Chile's Atacama Desert, corners of Bolivia's Altiplano, and Argentina's northwestern highlands. The northeast margin of the desert lies high on Andean slopes in Peru, along an inland contour where rainfall averages one inch a year. The desert air feels damp. It is damp because of the Peru Current. But when it

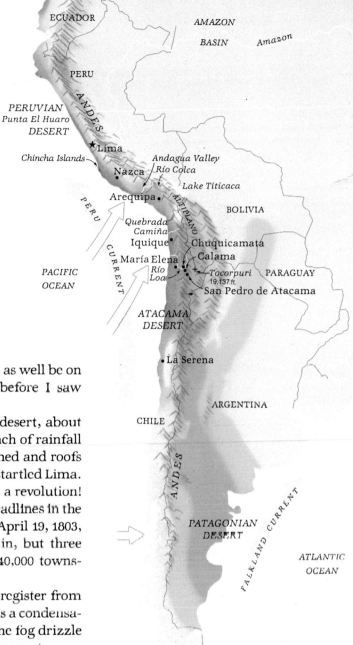

Wide ribbon of aridity follows South America's western coastline for 2,175 miles. The Peruvian and Atacama Deserts suffer from a rain-inhibiting temperature inversion— cold dense air underlying warm air—caused by the Peru Current's cooling effect. The Andes promote aridity by blocking moisture-bearing clouds rising from the Amazon Basin, thus leaving western slopes in a rain shadow. Farther south, the prevailing conditions reverse. The Andes bar rain from reaching the Patagonian Desert; the Atlantic's cold Falkland Current triggers a climatic inversion.

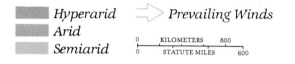

▮ *Hyperarid*	⇨ *Prevailing Winds*
▮ *Arid*	
▮ *Semiarid*	

```
0        KILOMETERS        800
0        STATUTE MILES          600
```

comes to honest rainfall, the desert coast of Chile and Peru might as well be on Mars. I spent nearly 5,000 days and nights on that seashore before I saw lightning, heard thunder, or needed an umbrella.

Yet freak thunderstorms may occur almost anywhere in this desert, about once a generation. They make history, because a fraction of an inch of rainfall causes great disturbances in a land where dry riverbeds are farmed and roofs resemble sieves. Before dawn on April 6, 1981, seven thunderbolts startled Lima. At first, people thought the flashes of sound were cannon fire . . . a revolution! Less than a tenth of an inch of rain made puddles in streets and headlines in the newspapers. I had to pore through history all the way back to April 19, 1803, before I could find a report of an earlier thunderstorm: no rain, but three lightning flashes around midnight that made some of Lima's 40,000 townspeople "flee in panic from a phenomenon never seen before."

Coastal meteorological stations in Peru and northern Chile register from zero to one inch of precipitation a year. Rarely rain, the moisture is a condensation of sea fog. Called *garúa* in Peru and *camanchaca* in Chile, the fog drizzle turns some hilltops green and changes sidewalk dust into slippery paste.

Most of the estimated ten million people who dwell in one of the driest of deserts are kept alive by rivers flowing down the western slopes of the Andes. In Peru alone during January and February—the months of greatest rainfall on the Andean summits—as many as 35 rivers cross the desert to the sea. By September the waters of scarcely ten rivers reach the Pacific.

Few river valleys exist in the Atacama Desert of northern Chile. Here the terrain levels out into a high expanse 500 miles long and far wider and flatter than any plain along the Peruvian coast. The Andean highlands of northern Chile are the most arid part of the range, primarily because they are so far removed from wet Amazon air masses. The amount of runoff that reaches the Pacific is small. One splendid exception is the Río Loa. This river makes a green loop through 275 thirsty miles before it gives up its last drops to the Pacific.

The easiest access to the desert region is the Pan American Highway. The asphalt Panamericana emerges from drought-resistant *(Continued on page 90)*

GEORG GERSTER (ABOVE)

Dampness and dryness meet along the coast of South America. At Punta El Huaro in Peru (left) a fist of the desert plunges into the sea. The same prevailing southerly winds that buffet surf off the point bring fog rather than rain to the Atacama Desert in Chile (top). The mantle of mist forms at sea when moisture in the Pacific air blows across the cold Peru Current and condenses. Above: Carved into a hillside on Peru's Península Paracas, the centuries-old Tres Cruces, or La Candelabra, faces seaward. Who made the design—and why—remains a mystery. Scientists, however, can identify the forces that carved the cliffs below it. Coastal uplift exposed the rocky shore to the erosive effects of waves.

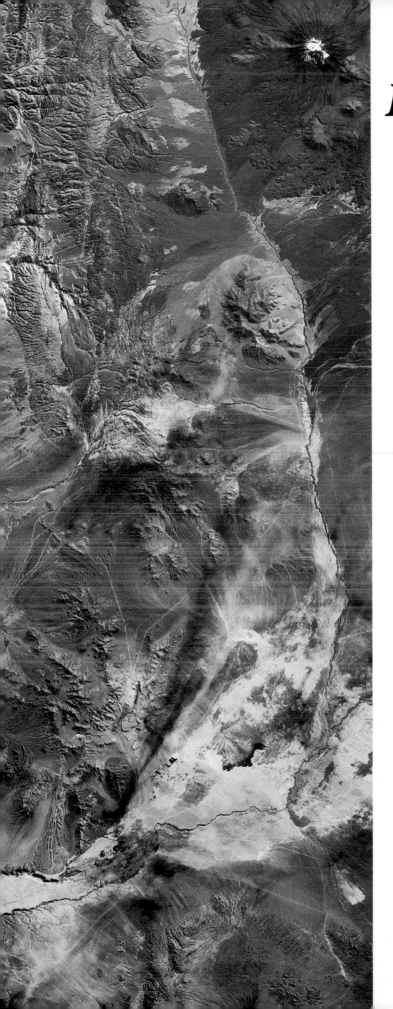

R*ío Loa leaves its signature on this Landsat image of rugged northern Chile (left). Beginning high in the peaks of the Andes, upper right, the river flows south, slices west across a plain, then descends through the Coastal Range to the Pacific Ocean, where fog hugs the coast, left. Vegetation along the Río Loa shows up in red. Trees and crops appear as a large red patch around Calama, a city of 92,500, in the lower right. Just above Calama lies the open-pit copper mine at Chuquicamata, one of the world's largest man-made holes. Extensive nitrate fields extend between the lower reaches of Río Loa and the coast. Below: In Chile, river valleys such as the Quebrada Camiña cradle small pockets of life in an otherwise desolate land. Agriculture here depends on irrigation.*

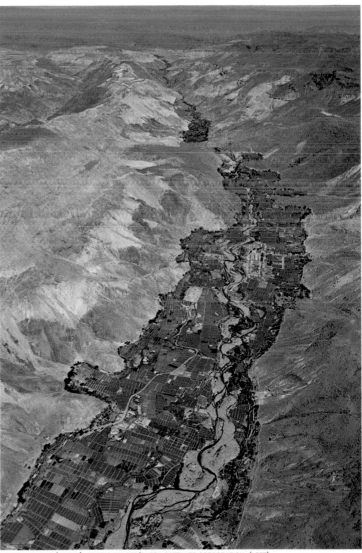

GEORG GERSTER (ABOVE); GEOPIC IMAGES/EARTH SATELLITE CORPORATION. (LEFT)

*H*ard-won bounty from an arid land demands labor, cooperation—and water. In Chile's Camiña river valley, mountain runoff collected in village canal systems irrigates plots of beans, maize, and alfalfa (right). In addition to subsistence farming, villagers raise small herds of sheep and goats for milk, cheese, and wool—the region's main export and source of cash. Below: The llama remains among man's best friends in the central Andes, where it has served as a beast of burden for several thousand years. Knitted ear tassels identify the animal's owner.

FOLLOWING PAGES: *Dust-covered hills in Chile's Atacama bear the scars of flash-flood erosion—evidence that rain, however rarely, does fall on this hyperarid desert.*

GEORG GERSTER (BOTH AND FOLLOWING PAGES)

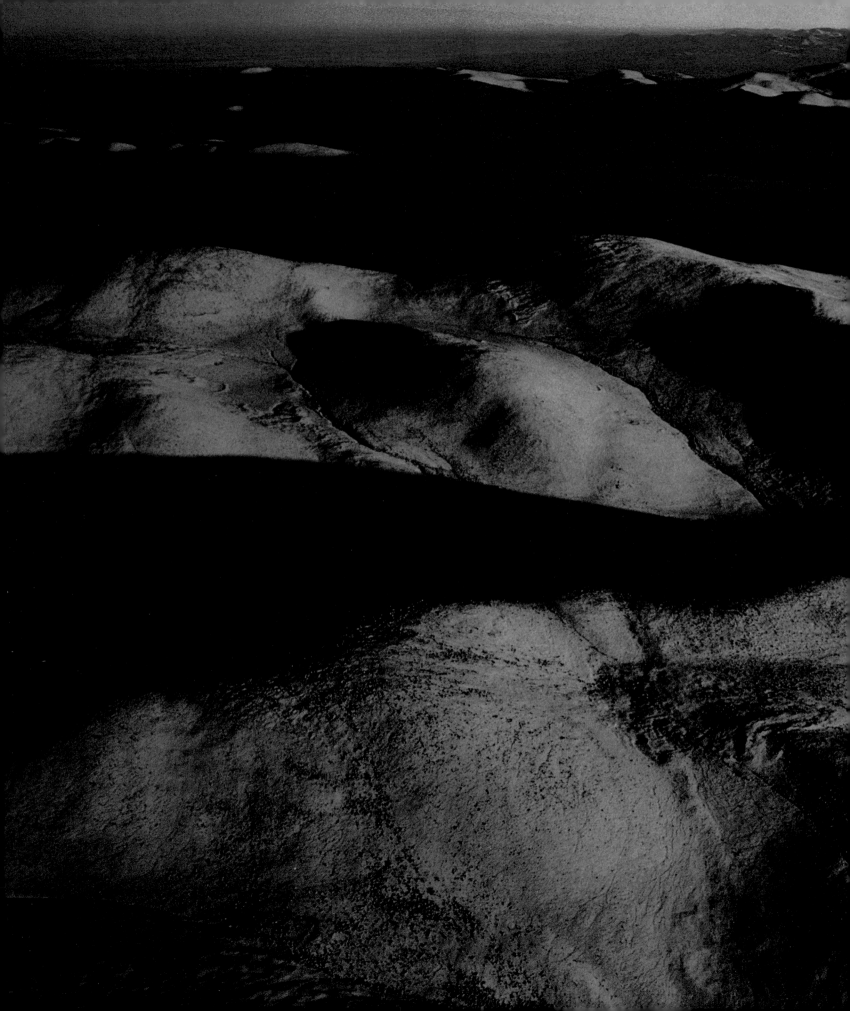

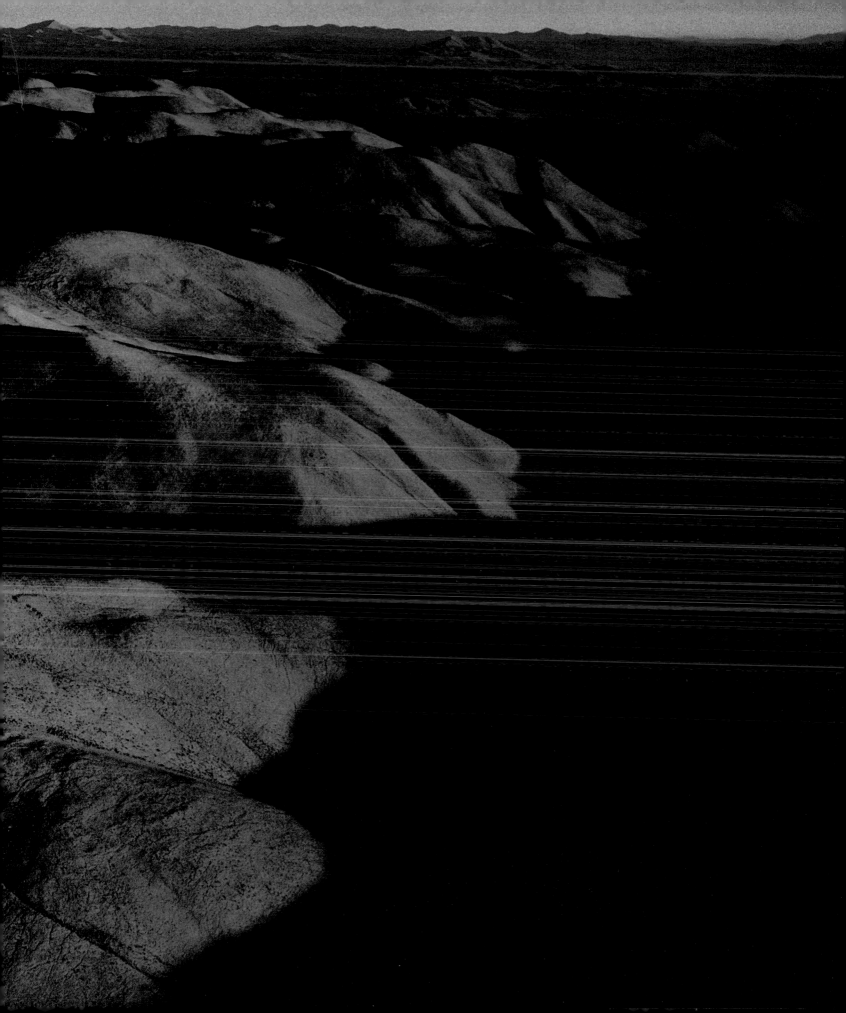

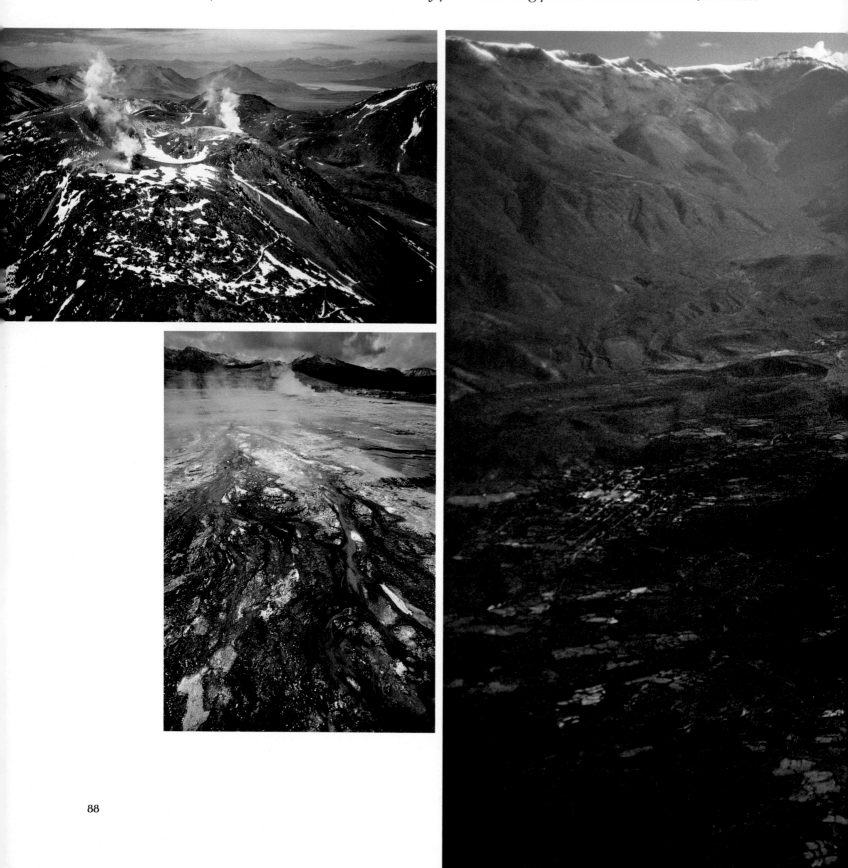

*T*win cinder cones taper above irrigated fields in Peru's Andagua valley, rimmed by the Andes. Molten rock, generated deep in the earth by colliding tectonic plates, formed these cones in relatively recent times. The same collisions of plates over long periods created the Andes, scientists believe. *Below, left: On the Atacama's eastern edge, the volcano Tocorpuri wears a cloak of golden sulfur produced by condensing gases. Bottom, left: Algae-rich mineral waters of Chile's Tatio geyser field dye the desert with colorful abstract patterns.*

forests below the Peru-Ecuador border and threads 2,600 dry miles to La Serena, Chile, where, shortly to the south, trees take up again. The route streaks over the open desert and always entices me to race across the empty stretches. Not even a bug splatters on my windshield. The wastelands, many with descriptive names, such as Llano de la Paciencia—Plains of Patience—occasionally reveal hints of human life. I see ski tracks slaloming down an enormous dune; messages of love or politics written on hillsides with tillandsia, a rootless plant that people pick up and arrange in letters and designs; or a single bright tent centered on a broad beach where a family is spending a week away from the city.

The Panamericana links all the riverine oases. Some 25 of these oases live by taking water from rivers that, as a result, dry up before they reach the sea. Most of the fertile wedges are pinched into deep gorges but widen at the rivers' mouths and spread up to ten miles across. Marigolds, cotton, rice, and sugarcane adorn the oases. Penetration roads climb from the Panamericana into the Andes along most of the watercourses.

I often drive the main highway eastward out of Lima. This important road is paved the entire 518 miles to a navigable Amazon tributary. Only ten miles out of town motorists emerge from the dank cloud that hovers monotonously over Lima for seven or eight midyear months. Twenty miles farther, travelers whiz through Chosica, a resort town that is bathed in sunshine and surrounded by bone-dry mountains.

The highway grows steeper and steeper, but not until the 10,000-foot-elevation mark is reached does enough natural vegetation grow to indicate that the desert at last has been left below. That touch of green soon gives way to bleak rock and glaciers at a 16,000-foot pass, one of the highest points along any highway in the world.

The trans-Andean roads and railways of northernmost Chile lead not into rain forest but into more desert: the Altiplano of southwestern Bolivia. There it rains a little, and sometimes hails furiously. The plain lies 12,000 feet above sea level and remains as flat as the prehistoric lake that once covered it. The lake evaporated, leaving a 5,000-square-mile salt flat. When I drive that chill white surface without horizon, I imagine I am snowmobiling on polar ice. To travel through this region of few filling stations, I have to carry enough gasoline to cross hundreds of miles.

Beyond the salt flat, the border of northeastern Chile seems to be drawn—like a child's connect-the-numbered-dot picture—from crater to crater through dozens of volcanoes. Some peaks approach 20,000 feet, the loftiest volcanoes on earth. Many are shaped like Japan's Fujiyama, little eroded, and some still fume. During a 1972 exploration of Inca highways, I learned that several summits hold Inca shrines. Child sacrifices—bodies frozen to death 500 years ago and preserved by the dry cold—have been found.

To revisit the volcanoes in February 1981, I turned off Chile's Panamericana and headed east toward Chuquicamata, a big mining town. The grade of the Atacama tilted so gently that I drove to 7,000 feet without noticing the climb. At Chuquicamata an open-pit copper mine measures 12,000 feet long and 1,420 feet deep, one of the world's largest man-made holes. On (Continued on page 94)

Landsat sensors record about a hundred miles of varied terrain in northern Chile, at one of the country's widest sections (opposite). Along the Bolivian border, upper right, snow-covered peaks of the Andes mingle with the royal blue brilliance of lakes slowly evaporating in the dry climate. The gray in the center of the image identifies the southern part of the Salar de Atacama, an immense salt flat in the Andean chain. Just above the salar, red shading reflects agriculture around the town of San Pedro de Atacama. The Cordillera Domeyko flanks the left side of the salar, and volcanic rocks appear in brown above San Pedro.

GEOPIC IMAGES/EARTH SATELLITE CORPORATION

In the Altiplano of Bolivia, a Chipaya Indian uses a digging stick (above) to plant seeds that yield a grain called quinua (left). Quinua thickens and adds protein to soups. Below: A hairstyle of elaborate braids dates back to ancient Chipaya forebears. Opposite: Sod huts shelter the Indians from dust storms and cold nights.

the brink of the mine I needed binoculars to get a good look at trucks loading ore on the bottom at the far end of the giant pit.

On the road 50 miles beyond Chuquicamata, long before I sighted the volcanoes, three big raindrops splattered on my windshield. Rain on the Atacama! I stopped and jumped out to take a picture of this rare event. *CRRACK*, a thunderbolt struck a salt flat so close that it rattled me. A fireball danced for a moment on the salt. The sizzle smelled of ozone.

I dived into the safety of my car just as the cloud burst. With windshield wipers slashing vainly at the downpour, I bored into the dark afternoon. Nearly an hour away was San Pedro de Atacama. The town held friends, a small hotel, and the finest archaeological museum in northern Chile.

I zigzagged through the "Valley of the Moon"—so-called because its landscape, eroded yet showing little runoff pattern, resembles the lunar surface. The weird landforms seemed to writhe under stabs of lightning and melt into the rust-red syrup that slopped hubcap deep across the highway. I sloshed into town, crossing the bridge a scant few minutes before it was engulfed by the Río San Pedro—normally a dry gulch. I called on my friend Roberto Sanchez amid a salvo of "Bolivian artillery," his name for thunderclaps. "These summer storms blow in from the east once or twice a decade. They bring Bolivian Winter, or *Invierno Boliviano,* as desert folks call it."

All that week thunderstorms prowled the region, striking at random, dumping hailstones and layering snow on volcanoes. The rain caused flooding in the northern part of the Salar de Atacama, watering down its reputation as one of the driest salt flats on earth.

I had read that it has never rained in Calama, so I left San Pedro for that Atacama city of 92,500. Orlando Rocha, chief of the government weather office in Calama, opened files for me. The records showed that it had rained in the city five of the past ten years and had snowed once. Total precipitation for the decade: 1½ inches, half of it in 1972.

"Is it fair to say that in some parts of the Atacama rain has never been recorded?" I asked Rocha.

He rolled his eyes upward. "A play on words. Obviously rain isn't recorded anywhere on earth where there's no rain gauge . . . and we have less than one hundred weather stations in northern Chile." He shrugged. "Yet *all* our stations have recorded *some* precipitation at *some* time. Keep this in mind: There are no regional rains along hundred-mile fronts; only sporadic cloudbursts. A cloudburst may lay an inch of water on a rain gauge or may miss it by a hundred meters. That makes for iffy averages."

He drew out charts showing that lower places tend to be drier. The coastal cities—Arica, Iquique, Antofagasta—go for years without recording so much as a tenth of a millimeter, about the thickness of this sheet of paper.

Although cloudbursts can be catastrophic, earthquakes are more feared. South America's west coast deserts lie along a portion of the Pacific ring of fire. Every coastal city and town has been hit by crustal violence; cemeteries hold tens of thousands of victims. About 50 times a century offshore quakes, sometimes as far away as Alaska, send tsunamis—seismic sea waves—against South America. But only about once a generation do waves, usually local in

origin, surge large enough to hurl ships ashore and to wipe out towns. Callao's worst tsunami struck in 1746. A wave about 60 feet high killed five to seven thousand people; two hundred survived.

Standing high above the water, many cliffs and ancient beaches are immune to tsunamis. Sections of the coast are rising a fraction of an inch a year. Some places emerge with earthquake jumps, while others subside. Land erodes into the sea. And vast amounts of seaside sand blow inland to cover the lower slopes of the Peruvian Andes with enormous dunes. In Chile the blowing sand is blocked from the Atacama plain by bluffs that rise as high as 3,000 feet directly behind the shore.

Atacama's hard earth looks useless, but its hidden riches—or seeming lack thereof—have caused two historic conflicts, which still cloud the relationship between Chile and Peru. The first fracas erupted in 1537 after Pizarro conquered the Incas. He sent his partner, Diego de Almagro, and 570 Spaniards into the Atacama to seek gold. The "Men of Chile" returned so disillusioned that they rebelled, seized part of Peru, and eventually murdered Pizarro.

Then in 1879 one of South America's fiercest conflicts, the War of the Pacific, began when Chile captured the northern Atacama from Bolivia and then overran Peru. Some writers call it the "Salitre War" because it contested the ownership of mines yielding salitre—sodium nitrate. The substance was first used for manufacturing gunpowder and later for making fertilizer. The

Lightning heralds a thunderstorm moving toward the lunar landscape of the "Valley of the Moon" in northern Chile (above and opposite, top). Local cloudbursts, infrequent in this area, can unleash disaster. Much of the rainfall does not penetrate the crusty soil; it runs off, causing flash floods that pool in low-lying areas such as the Plains of Patience (opposite, bottom).

nitrate is processed from caliche, a water-soluble mineral deposit that in a wetter climate would dissolve. A layer of caliche generally several feet thick lies just under the Atacama surface. The mineral layer extends 200 miles north and just as far south of María Elena, one of two nitrate plants—*oficinas*—I found still functioning in Chile in 1981.

A María Elena employee, Jorge Montecinos, told me that scientists aren't sure where caliche comes from. "Some surmise organic origins, from the sea. Others think minerals were washed down from the mountains, or seeped up from the subsoil, or came from nitric acid released by violent lightning storms that were spawned when hundreds of volcanoes to the east erupted," Jorge said. George E. Ericksen of the U.S. Geological Survey believes that caliche was formed by windblown salts from diverse sources. The process is so slow, he says, that it has taken 10 or 15 million years of extreme aridity to permit commercial thicknesses of caliche to form.

Shipments of nitrate to England and the United States for making fertilizer and gunpowder began in the 1830s. The white crystals probably helped propel bullets in the Crimean War and at Bull Run. Around 1859 demand for salitre in agriculture burgeoned. By the 1920s the Chilean budget depended mainly upon the income from duty on nitrate exports.

Then came the Great Depression. Sixty thousand men, two-thirds of the salitre work force, were laid off by 1931. Synthetic nitrogen fertilizers had invaded the market. Oficinas became ghost towns overnight.

The two remaining oficinas produce 600,000 tons of sodium nitrate a year and 20 percent of the world's iodine. Strewn up and down the Panamericana for hundreds of miles stand the remains of other oficinas. Some have been declared national monuments. The Chileans call them *cementerios*—cemeteries of rusty iron, crumbling adobe shacks, and teetering bandstands.

Near the abandoned plants rise artificial buttes: flat-topped hills, the tailings from salitre processing. Touring one ghost oficina, I heard a disintegrating iron smokestack rumbling in the wind, like distant gunfire. The muffled sound called to mind the thousands of ragtag soldiers who had fought and died on this arid plain in the War of the Pacific a century ago.

Like salitre, guano is a fertilizer whose accumulation depends on lack of rainfall. Unlike salitre, guano is a renewable resource: excrement of seabirds, rich in nitrogen, potassium, and phosphorus. As a fertilizer, guano is three to seven times more effective than barnyard manure.

I remember visiting one rookery in the 1950s on North Chincha, a flat-topped island off the Peruvian shore. Over the ground stretched a living blanket of birds: thousands of guanayes and some pelicans and boobies. Black-jacketed, white-breasted guanayes, or Peruvian cormorants, waddled around on short legs, rather like penguins, snatching tail feathers from one another to add to their bowl-shaped nests of white excrement.

Guano birds were long Peru's best money-makers. Diving into the cold sea to gulp anchovies, the birds would return to their nests and regurgitate their catch to feed their young. Mineral-rich guano slowly accumulated around the nests. As much as 20 million tons of it had encrusted offshore islands by the 1840s. Merchants became aware of it, and soon fleets of foreign sailing ships arrived. Around the Chincha Islands alone, dozens of vessels rode at anchor, waiting with open holds for gunnysacks stinking of ammonia. The sacks were filled by hapless guano workers, many of them Chinese coolies, emaciated, their backs creased by slave-drivers' whips. Many Chinese committed suicide. At one time their corpses could be found at the foot of the cliffs, mummified in the guano.

By 1910 the deposits were all but gone. Peru acted to protect the birds. By mid-century the leading authority on South American oceanic birds, Dr. Robert Cushman Murphy, reported that in peak years 90 million birds were feeding on some ten trillion anchovies annually—more fish than all the known stars in our galaxy. The food chain of the Peru Current is short and stable, and its major links are nutrients, plankton, anchovies, and guano birds, Dr. Murphy observed. But he warned in the March 1959 NATIONAL GEOGRAPHIC that anchovies "are vanishing into a vast new maw, factories that grind them into fish meal for cattle and poultry food."

He also described a natural threat: "A warm deadly current from the tropics, called *El Niño* — The Child — because it usually appears near the Christmas season, sometimes surges southward along the coast, heating cool ocean waters. . . . Havoc results. Marine life perishes. Hydrogen sulfide bubbles as a putrefactive product from the sick sea."

Despite protests from ecologists and the guano industry, more than one hundred fishmeal factories were soon putting out bad odors and good profits. Peru led the world's fisheries in tonnage. By 1970 the anchovy catch totaled 27 billion pounds, one sixth of all fish caught in all the waters on earth. Their food supply depleted, the weakened guanayes fell prey to disease. Some birds died in flight. The sea threw their carcasses onto beaches, often hip deep.

Then El Niño struck. By 1973 — the year Dr. Murphy died, his warning unheeded — the anchovy catch had decreased 87 percent. The drop in worldwide protein supply forced farmers in many countries to raise soybeans as a fishmeal substitute. The ecological cycle dependent on the Peru Current had been knocked askew, if not ruined.

In 1981 I saw little more than stray feathers in the once-crowded rookeries, although I eventually found about 50,000 guanayes nesting in a hidden place in the south, and more on a distant island in the north. I recalled Dr. Murphy's description of the prodigality of wildlife when I was very young: "Picture to yourself . . . dark flocks of guanayes [forming] rafts . . . gobbling up fish in their path, the hinder margins of the rafts . . . pouring over the van in some such manner as . . . passenger pigeons . . . once rolled through American forests." He chose a fateful comparison, since the last passenger pigeon died in 1914.

Guano beds once measured up to 150 feet thick. Guano has been estimated to accumulate several feet a century. The earliest deposits were formed perhaps 5,000 years ago when rainfall slackened. "Gold and silver ornaments, stone carvings, wood figures, pottery, and textiles have been found embedded as deep as 60 feet," Dr. Murphy reported. The oldest relics found date to A.D. 400, the time of the Moche, one of the great early civilizations in Peru. The Moche visited the guano islands to worship and to hunt sea lions.

Aridity of coastal Peru and northern Chile has slowed the decay of mummies and artifacts dating back to communities that *(Continued on page 100)*

F. GOHIER/PHOTO RESEARCHERS, INC.

Saucers of bunchgrass known locally as paja brava *dot a plateau in the Chilean Andes. The growth begins as a single clump. As it exhausts nutrients from the soil, the vegetation sends out a circle of new growth. Top: A cardon cactus, a source of wood and fruit, clutches rocky ground in the Atacama.*

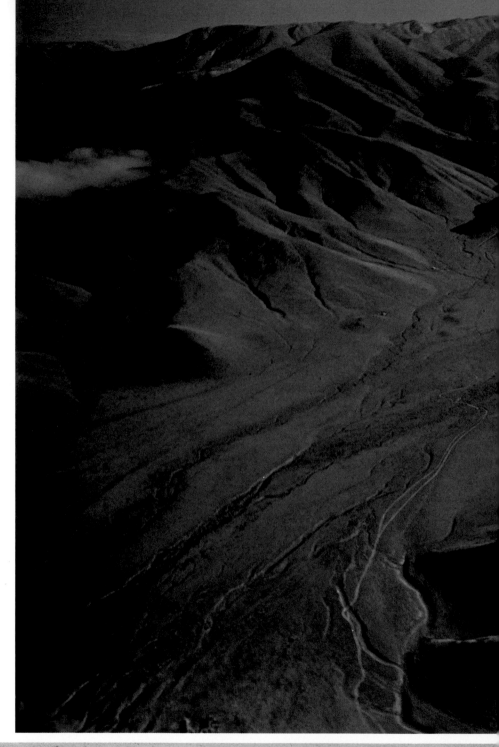

*G*reen herbaceous plant life carpets foothills in the Andes of Peru (right). At elevations of 1,000 to 2,000 feet, heavy fog nourishes the vegetation. Herds of sheep and goats trail up to the hills to feed during the winter. When overgrazing or a shrinking fog cover depletes the open pastures, shepherds move animals to cultivated fields along river valleys (below). Some herdsmen seek out grazing land higher in the Peruvian Andes, where summer rains bring the land to life.

Four Humboldt penguins, one a double-banded mutant, peer out to sea from a high cliff. Unlike species living closer to Antarctica, these penguins nest in burrows dug in guano, or bird excrement, to avoid overheating. When fertilizer companies stripped away the guano, Humboldt penguins no longer burrowed in large numbers and today travelers see few of them.

stacked seashells near the beaches 7,000 years ago. Today pockmarks of countless graves ransacked by gold seekers scar the broad pampas and hidden valleys. Most of the dug-up loot has been melted down, and the mummies and textiles have been cast aside to shrivel in the sun. Even so, museums and private collections bulge with millions of fine examples of pre-Columbian art—mostly ceramics—from South America's west coast desert. So numerous were the ancient potters that some coastal cemeteries are practically paved with shards. The sands still conceal untold treasures and secrets of mysterious civilizations.

Not concealed are the Nazca lines in southern Peru. Here on the dry pampa a puzzle is laid out for all the world to ponder. From the air, travelers grasp the grand proportions of the lines, which form geometric and zoomorphic designs on the desert floor. Nazca people created the patterns 1,500 to 2,000 years ago. By removing black rocks and exposing the lighter undersurface of the desert, the ancients created intricate patterns. My longtime friend Maria Reiche has been studying the perplexing designs most of her life. But neither she nor archaeologists have concluded what the lines mean.

I assisted Maria with her studies again in 1981. I first wrote about her in the May 1975 NATIONAL GEOGRAPHIC. Maria has since become one of Peru's tourist attractions. Now 78 and going blind, Maria no longer sleeps on the desert in a nest of old tape measures. With free room and board provided for the rest of her life by the government hotel at Nazca, Maria holds daily conferences with visitors from many nations.

"My Nazca book sells like hotcakes, but I have little personal use for money," she told me. The quintessential desert rat, she was carelessly dressed in the same clothes she'd worn a year earlier. "All my earnings go to pay and equip four motorcycle guards who keep vehicles from tracking up the desert."

Maria berates anyone who dares to turn over a single pebble, lest some record of the past be lost. The rain cloud hanging over my head that year didn't help. It brought her grave distress: a rare downpour. Maria stayed up all one April night wringing her hands. "I dread that a deluge may wash out the lines before I've finished mapping them," she cried.

A look from the air next day revealed no damage. The ancient erosion patterns—both under and over the designs—were still deeply etched. Maria need not worry; the climate seems as dry as ever, with little change in sight.

What is changing, however, is the greening of the desert in some places. On the Atacama near Pozo Almonte, Chile, I was surprised to find straight rows of *tamarugos*, a type of mesquite, spread for miles across the gnarled crust of the salt flats. Nurtured by man at first, the trees now draw their own subsurface water through roots of surprising length. The normal maximum length of the roots is 40 feet. The tamarugos produce clusters of thin seedpods that are prized as a food source for livestock because of their high protein content.

When the atomic age began, scientists foresaw water for coastal deserts coming from seawater desalinized by nuclear energy. Now another plan is under way to cultivate the Pampa de Majes. Amazon headwaters will be diverted to this south Peruvian desert through tunnels high in the Andes. Six nations—Peru, Sweden, the United Kingdom, Spain, Canada, and South

Sea lions swim and fur seals sun along Peru's coast. Nutrients circulating up from the depths just offshore foster minute plant life, called phytoplankton. Small fish feed on these tiny organisms and form a critical link in the short food chain that ultimately supports an array of sea mammals and birds.

Africa—have already spent half a billion dollars to drill 62 miles of tunnels for irrigating 140,268 acres of desert. The project will draw water from the Río Colca high in the Andes and channel it to fertile soil below. A bonus will be hydroelectric power for southern Peruvian mines and cities, which now depend on diesel generators for 83 percent of their electricity.

In 1981, on the day water first flowed through the system, I called on Nils Ellström of Stockholm at his office in Arequipa, a city at the base of a 19,000-foot volcano. Ellström was head of the Majes Project. "I've built tunnels all around the world," he said. "But never in such a spectacular site as this. Drilling through the Andes is an engineer's nightmare but a geologist's dream. Imagine walking into the middle of a rocky mountain, passing a layer of seashells here, a layer of ash there. But what I like best is the prospect of raising food for people of the future, and the excitement of creating a city in the wasteland."

A wasteland? Not altogether, I thought, as I flew from Arequipa to Lima. Those unforgettable patterns of dunes and coastal ranges would never have been created had rains often fallen. Ironically the very aridity that embittered the Men of Chile 450 years ago has proved to be a most precious asset. Temples, textiles, and 7,000-year-old foodstuffs of the people who preceded Pizarro would never have been preserved but for the rainlessness. Nitrates—of such worth that thousands died for the right to mine them—would have been leached away in a wetter climate. Guano that fertilized the fields of Europe and the United States never could have accumulated. I thought about the great open-pit copper mines, Cuajone in Peru and Chuquicamata in Chile, and about the open-pit iron mines—Marcona in Peru and El Tofo in Chile. As with nitrates their dross is strewn in man-made mountains on the sand while their essence is spirited away to other lands.

Gold, silver, copper, iron, salitre, iodine ... millions of tons have been shipped from South America to Yokohama, Liverpool, Antwerp, Cádiz, Portland, Baltimore, and scores of other seaports. Many nations, including the United States, have used this yield for display in museums, for building factories, and for fertilizing their soil to enrich the food supply.

Possibly we all carry a trace of South America's coastal deserts within us, in body or mind. I know I do.

Squawking flocks of cormorants, boobies, and pelicans echo a time when millions of seabirds nested along Peru's coast. Their numbers declined when El Niño, *a warm current from the north, invaded the area. Then, overfishing of anchovies by purse seiners, such as the one offshore, further reduced the birds' sole food source. At one time thick layers of guano—mineral-rich excrement on the nesting grounds—gave Peru a major fertilizer resource. But companies loading thousands of ships a year stripped the rookeries of the valuable deposit. Below: Neck-deep in its parent's gullet, a young cormorant gulps down a fresh-caught anchovy.*

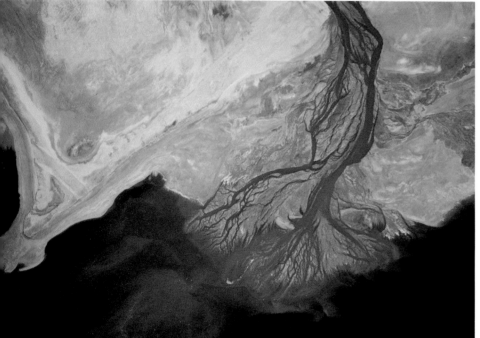

*S*pecter *from more prosperous times, abandoned Santa Laura (right) glows ghostlike in the desert sunset. From the 1830s to the 1930s such plants, called* oficinas, *processed the Atacama's wealth of sodium nitrate, once a principal fertilizer raw material. Synthetic fertilizers undercut the market and now only two* oficinas *operate. Railroad cars from one of the plants deliver sodium sulfate—used in detergents and in paper processing (top). Above: At Chuquicamata, copper tailings stain the desert. The Atacama holds the world's largest known copper deposits.*

*A*ncient puzzle, the Nazca lines etch a plateau in southern Peru (left). People made the designs 1,500 to 2,000 years ago by removing dark surface stones to expose light ground beneath. Since 1949 Maria Reiche (top) has tried to interpret the etchings. To study the shapes, she and her assistant Benedita Morón cut the patterns out of paper (above). One line poses no mystery: The Pan American Highway arcs in the distance.

PRECEDING PAGES: *Relatively constant southerly winds whip dunes into complex shapes just inland from Peru's coast.*

Land of the Great Sand Seas

The Sahara of North Africa

By Tor Eigeland

Ancient stock exchange: In the midst of turbaned nomads, a skull-capped Mozabite merchant sizes up sheep as trading activity dominates the marketplace in Ghardaïa. The Algerian town prospers as the centuries-old capital of the M'zab, an oasis region in the Sahara, the world's largest desert.

PIERRE BOULAT

A distant gleam across the flat pebble desert caught my eye. It was just a brief flash in the cold January dawn of northern Africa, and I saw no more until our old Peugeot had rattled much closer on the bumpy dirt track. "Look!" I exclaimed to my companion, Morocco-based Austrian photographer Heinz Klaus. "What's that boy doing sitting by his bicycle in the middle of nowhere?"

We were in the Moroccan part of the Sahara, traveling eastward from Erfoud. Behind us the snowcapped peaks of the High Atlas Mountains reached into the winter sky. Ahead of us lay the Algerian border. There was no settlement in sight, not even a nomad's tent.

Huddled and shivering, wrapped in an old jacket with a woolen cap drawn over his eyes, a Berber boy of about 12 attempted to smile as we approached. His outstretched hands held something.

"Fossile, monsieur?" he croaked in a morning-rough voice. He was selling petrified goniatites, long-extinct spiral-shelled mollusca, faintly related to the present-day chambered nautilus. Secretive about where they find them, local tribesmen dig out what look like plain rocks, chip them to expose the fossil, which they polish to bring out the lovely snail-like shape of the goniatite.

Alone and cold, the poor but proud Berber boy selling marine fossils presented a touching image. Like just about every living thing in the Sahara, he has to struggle to survive. Though the boy was hardly aware of it, the goniatites he sold dated back to a time about 400 million years ago when vast reaches of the Sahara were covered by water. After the sea creatures lost their bid for existence, the water receded, and the seafloor became dry land.

Today the world's biggest desert, the Sahara spreads across nearly 3½ million square miles—roughly the size of the United States. Representing the western end of the Afro-Asian desert zone, the Sahara rules from the Red Sea westward across the wide brow of North Africa and down the southeastern slopes of the Saharan Atlas Mountains to the Atlantic. In the south a region called the Sahel separates the sprawling desert from the moist tropics. Fewer than two million nomads live in the Sahara. Except for the Nile River Valley, only 780 square miles of oases carry sufficient water to support agriculture.

The Sahara is a frightening place of scorching heat and numbing cold, flash floods and sandstorms. Ground temperature has reached 183°F at Tamanrasset, a town in southern Algeria, and the air temperature has fallen to 5°F in the Tibesti Mountains of northwestern Chad. On the other hand, the Sahara embraces startling beauty. It can jar one's emotions with the overpowering silence of its brilliant, star-studded night sky. The loveliness of a reddish dawn or sunset in the wide open spaces can inspire a joyous feeling of freedom, making the desert nomad shout a song at the top of his lungs as he rides his camel or—just as likely today—races his Japanese pickup truck through the sand. Sahara in Arabic appropriately means "deserts," because deserts they are: gravel, boulder, mountain, and salt. Dune fields account for only some 20 percent of the surface. The Sahara's lowest point lies 436 feet below sea level in the huge Qattara Depression in Egypt's Western Desert. Highest elevations occur in the central mountains, the Ahaggar range in Algeria that peaks at 9,573 feet and the Tibesti mountains in northwestern Chad that soar to 11,204 feet at Emi Koussi. In between are lowlands and higher plains, the flat scorched surface stretching as far as the eye can see. I tried to imagine this barren landscape when it abounded with life 7,000 years ago, during one of the less arid periods of the Sahara. Cypress, oak, lime, alder, and olive trees grew on the grassy uplands. Roaming this paradise were elephants, giraffes, rhinoceroses, gazelles, and ostriches. Crocodiles, hippopotamuses, and fish stirred the waters of lakes and rivers, where only a few pools, dry lakes, and dry riverbeds known as wadis now exist.

Bones and other remains record the story, but the rock pictures that people carved, ground, and painted from the Atlas Mountains to the Nile Valley survive as one of the marvelous testimonies to earlier life in the Sahara. Uncounted thousands of splendid pictures exist on the Tassili-n-Ajjer plateau in southeastern Algeria. One of the most celebrated sites is Jabbaren. An area measuring 600 yards long by 600 yards wide, it displays more than 500 scenes. Done in various styles and sizes, the rock-art images, layered one atop the other, record the activities of various people who lived here at different times over a period of thousands of years.

Getting to the plateau requires a muscle-numbing climb up steep ravines and canyons from a level roughly 4,000 feet above sea level to a tableland at 7,000 feet. The setting alone is worth the visit. This fantasy world resembles a bizarre rock city drawn by a cartoonist. There are avenues, alleys, plazas, and cathedral-shaped stones sculpted by time. Complementing the scenery are a hundred or so gnarled cypresses that have miraculously clung to life since the

Blanketing almost the entire northern third of Africa, the Sahara envelops an area nearly equal in size to the United States. The desert stretches 3,000 miles from the Atlantic Ocean eastward to the Red Sea and extends more than 1,000 miles from the Atlas Mountains of Morocco and Algeria southward into the Sahel region, which borders tropical Africa. Barren plains and giant seas of shifting sand surround ancient mountains, including the Ahaggar, Aïr, Tibesti, Ennedi, and Tassili. The Sahara, from an Arabic word meaning "deserts," spreads across the borders of ten nations.

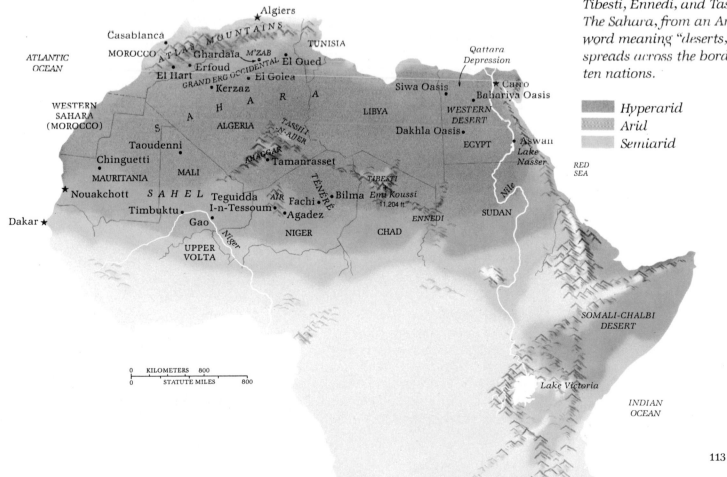

Hyperarid
Arid
Semiarid

prehistoric moist period. Perhaps three or four thousand years old, the trees stand as some of the world's oldest organisms. The Tassili rock engravings, discovered by a French desert patrol in 1848, have endured even longer than the cypresses. The initial images were carved into the pale reddish sandstones before 6000 B.C. The last were painted close to the Christian era, when the region had turned into desert.

Scholars use several sets of labels in classifying the pictures. The earliest engravings belong to the Large Wild Fauna—Bubalian—or Hunter period. The hunter lived here from about 7000 to 5000 B.C. The oldest images include hippopotamuses, rhinoceroses, giraffes, and giant buffaloes, often done larger than life size. People appear occasionally, wearing animal masks or armed with clubs in hunting scenes. Other images, painted in the Round Head style, show men with large, bulbous, featureless heads.

Most brilliant to me was the work done during the Herdsman, or Bovidian, period between 5000 and 2000 B.C. Smaller than the earlier images, the paintings show hunting and fighting with bows and arrows, dancing, and details of domestic life. But the most prominent subjects of the paintings of this period are domestic cattle—whole herds, along with goats, sheep, and dogs.

The creators of these scenes were skilled artists. They made their paints from ground ocher and white kaolin, and they brought their world to life with elegance, vigor, imagination, and rich colors. One can almost hear the cattle lowing, the herders shouting.

According to rock pictures of the Horse, or Equidian, period strangers—possibly Berbers from Libya—came to Tassili about 1200 B.C. Paintings show tunic-clad men in horse-drawn chariots—the legs of the horses stretching straight out to indicate flying gallop. Paintings found elsewhere suggest that the charioteers' route ran from the Mediterranean coast through the Tassili, the Ahaggar, and then down to Gao, a town on the Niger River in eastern Mali. The chariots appear to have been used in battle, for hunting, and possibly in races.

Slowly, the climate grew drier. With big game apparently gone, the artists drew smaller animals, such as antelopes, wild mountain sheep, and small lions. Then about 50 B.C. a new animal—the camel—appeared on the walls of Tassili. At first, camel paintings reflected the high quality of an earlier time, but soon degenerated into childlike depictions of oases and camel caravans.

The paid protectors of those caravans were the proud, tall Tuareg—ferocious raiders and warriors who controlled large parts of the Sahara. The famous blue-robed men of the desert may be descendants of the conquerors who ride across the rock canvas of Tassili's Horse period.

Today about 500,000 Tuareg live in the Sahara and the Sahel. Minimal requirements are the key to their survival. They rove from pasture to pasture with camels, goats, sheep, and, in the south, cattle. The Tuareg subsist mainly on a diet of milk, butter, and cheese. Tea, sugar, cloth, and blankets are acquired from merchants. Traditionally, the Tuareg obtained millet and dates from oases where their vassals cultivated the land in return for protection.

With a local guide, Hamdawi Abdel Rahman, I visited a Tuareg camp near Algeria's Assekrem, a 9,573-foot peak. *(Continued on page 120)*

Graceful curves of sand burnished by the morning sun sweep past a herder (opposite). His goats search for grass near the oasis of Kerzaz in Algeria's Grand Erg Occidental. Such dune fields make up only about one-fifth of the 3½ million square miles of the Sahara. The remaining reaches consist of sand and gravel plains, rocky plateaus, salt flats, and dry mountains.

KAZUYOSHI NOMACHI/PHOTO RESEARCHERS, INC.

GEORGE HOLTON/OCELOT

PIERRE BOULAT

THOMAS J. ABERCROMBIE, NATIONAL GEOGRAPHIC STAFF

*B*urnt crust from the Sahara oven, blackened spires of rock rise above the Tassili-n-Ajjer plateau of southeastern Algeria (top). Iron and manganese in the sandstone oxidize and harden to form the dark patina. Nearly barren today, the plateau preserves fragments of past life. Between 7000 and 1000 B.C., a succession of peoples lived on the highland during a moist period, when vegetation of the Mediterranean area flourished here. Rock paintings on Tassili walls depict hunting and herding (above). The white dots on the paired human figures resemble scar ornamentation still used by some African tribes. Left: Gnarled cypresses that have survived from the moist period draw water through huge roots sunk deep in a Tassili ravine. About 100 trees remain, their seeds unable to germinate in the rocky soil.

117

Dry highs, damp lows: The Atakor range of southern Algeria's Ahaggar Mountains thrusts arid peaks nearly 7,000 feet above sea level. Jagged cones of ancient volcanoes jut above a landscape inhabited only by nomadic Tuareg. The once powerful warriors attribute personalities to different parts of the mountains and weave stories about the imagined exploits of the various crags. Opposite: The Sahara drops to its lowest point—436 feet below sea level—in the Qattara Depression of northern Egypt. Salt marshes, rock salt, and sand and gravel cover the 7,500-square-mile basin.

PIERRE BOULAT (ABOVE); THOMAS J. ABERCROMBIE, NATIONAL GEOGRAPHIC STAFF (BELOW).

Low tents sheltered three women, a young man, and a few children. The youngest of the women, attractive, with braids and green makeup, informed us that since they could no longer find pasture many of the Tuareg had traveled several hundred miles to the west—to an area almost inaccessible by car. Others had gone south to the Republic of Niger. "We have stayed here," she said, "because our husbands have found work as laborers in Tamanrasset." This young woman, named Tuarik, showed us a tiny spring of trickling water and pointed out a few scrawny goats and sheep. Clearly not enough for survival. She said that her husband and those of the other women returned from time to time with food and supplies.

The Tuareg life-style resembles that of the nomadic Bedouin, with one big difference. These women were unveiled. Cheerfully chatting away, they entertained us in one of their open-flapped tents. In my 20 years of experience with the Bedouin, I had never seen this happen.

Their faces full of expression, the women spoke of the drought and of their families. Hamdawi translated what he thought suitable for my ears and conveyed news of other Tuareg to the women. His head and mouth, unlike the women's, were hidden by a white cloth, and his eyes were concealed behind dark glasses. Among the Tuareg, the man wears the veil. Called a *tagilmust,* it is both a turban and a veil—a cloth up to 20 feet long. Wrapped around the head and the face, it leaves only a slit for the eyes.

The most plausible reason for this startling reversal of who wears the veil is that during month-long camel caravans or raids in the desert, the men became accustomed to wearing the tagilmust as protection from wind, sand, heat, and cold. A dark blue veil will also cut the sun's glare. Another explanation for the tagilmust is more amusing but less likely. Many years ago, legend says, the women wore veils. But one day an enemy tribe mounted a surprise attack on a Tuareg camp, and the men, unprepared to fight, fled. Left behind, the women managed to organize a defense and after a furious battle drove off the attackers. In honor of the women it was decided they no longer had to wear veils, but the men had to cover their faces in shame.

The relative freedom the women enjoy may be the reason for the name of the tribe. Tuareg is a slightly twisted Arabic word that means "godforsaken." Traditional Arabs jealously guard their women and keep them in the background; the Tuareg, however, permit their women a free life until they marry. And this is often in their mid-twenties. On moonlit nights far from any town, unmarried men and women hold the *ahal*—a love feast of music, drumming, and recital of poetry. As the moon slips below the horizon, couples stroll off into the desert with ideas not purely spiritual.

Driving back toward Tamanrasset one afternoon, Hamdawi insisted we stop by a spring. Just like Bedouin, he delights in pointing out water sources. Water seeping from the ground had formed a small, slow-flowing creek. Tadpoles wriggled and small fish darted about in pools carved out of the surrounding rock. A few hundred yards downstream the creek dried out. It seemed a miracle of survival to find fish in the middle of the desert.

It reminded me of an even stranger find that Jacques Couëlle had reported to me in Paris a few weeks earlier. Couëlle, a world-famous architect, ecologist,

TOR EIGELAND (BOTH)

and member of the Academie Française des Beaux-Arts, had a crew dig a well in the desert near El Golea. The work was part of a study for a tourist development project. At a depth of about 130 feet the men struck brackish water. Strangely, it was stirring, churning. Puzzled, the crew returned the next day with baskets to trap whatever might be there—and found themselves pulling out fish.

"They were like tench and mullet," Couëlle said, "and completely blind—with only a membrane where there used to be eyes. They have reproduced under the desert, surviving for more than 10,000 years. There are hundreds of thousands of them, perhaps millions under the desert! We cooked some of the fish, and they were delicious."

We left the spring and continued toward Tamanrasset. "Life is getting very difficult for the Tuareg now," Hamdawi said. "The drought is terrible. Many have lost all their animals. And now we also have all these borders. Political borders. Before, we were free. We could go wherever we wanted. Sometimes our caravans lasted for three months."

"Are there still caravans?" I asked.

"No," Hamdawi said. "There are almost none now in Algeria. Before, you took the dates by camel from I-n-Salah to Niger. And from Niger, you took millet. Now it is prohibited to take things to Niger, and goods from Niger cannot come to Algeria."

From a dirt track we turned south, our tires singing on the hardtop Trans-Saharan highway just north of Tamanrasset. An important reason for the decline of the camel caravans was evident here. *(Continued on page 128)*

Bou Noura, which means "the luminous one," nestles in the M'zab valley of northern Algeria (above). Mozabites, members of a Muslim sect fleeing persecution in the 11th century, built the fortress town. Fired by religious zeal and a talent for commerce, they turned part of the wilderness into a lush garden. Today as then, Mozabites guard their privacy behind city walls. Opposite: In a timeless tableau, a farmer passes a covered archway in a M'zab town.

121

KAZUYOSHI NOMACHI/PHOTO RESEARCHERS, INC.

Driven by the wind, dunes advance on Kerzaz, Algeria, and stinging sand lashes a palm grove. Oasis dwellers

depend on palms for food, fuel, oil for cooking, rope, building materials, and shade.

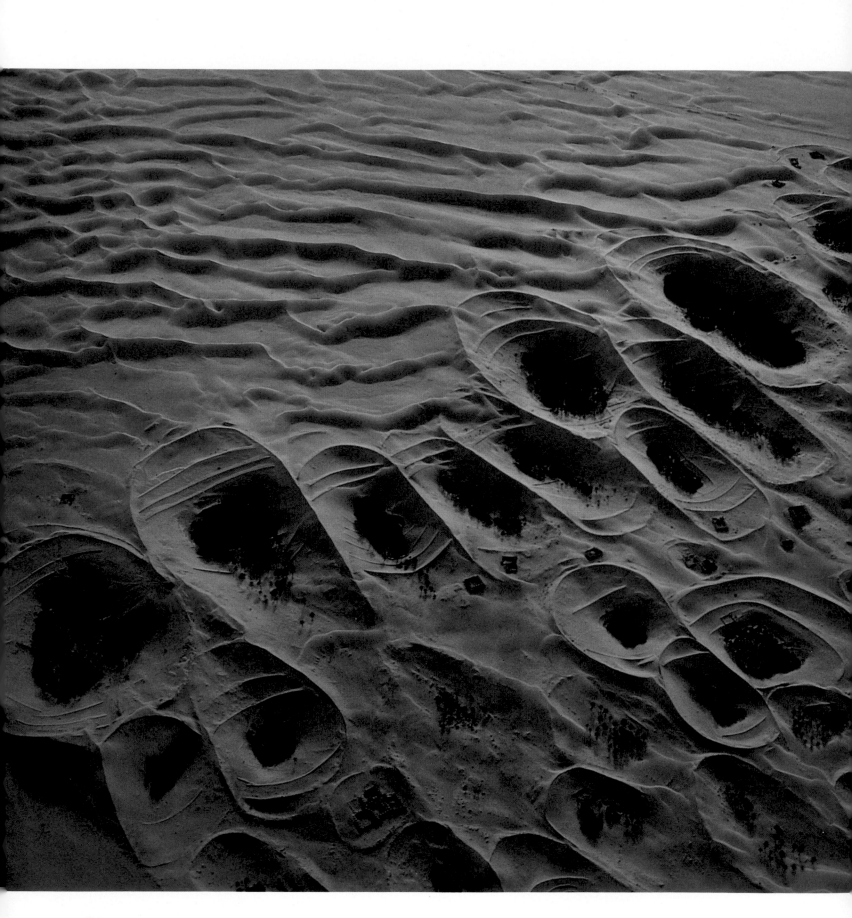

GEORG GERSTER (ALL)

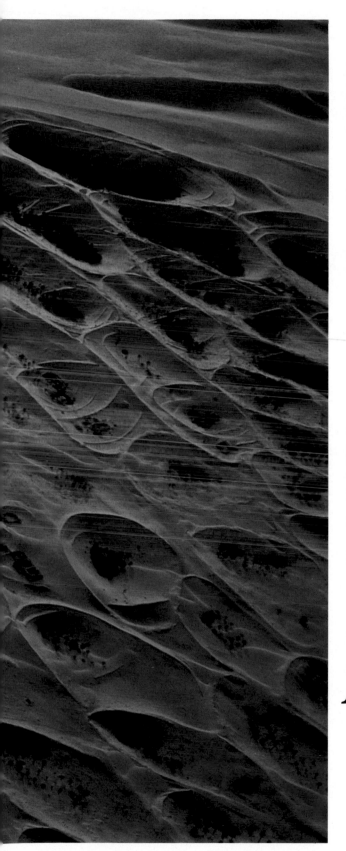

*R*esembling imprints of giant sandals, man-made craters
carved from the sand hold palm groves at El Oued in the Souf
region of northeastern Algeria (left). Growing from a pit in the side
of one of the crater oases, a young tree spreads above the stone
collar of a retaining wall (top). Owners dig the deep holes to place
the date palms closer to groundwater. Above: At market, shoppers
select fresh squash and melons grown in grove-shaded gardens.

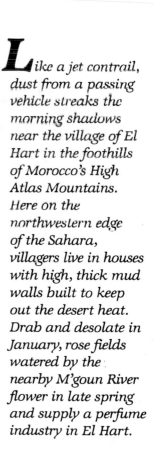

*L*ike a jet contrail, dust from a passing vehicle streaks the morning shadows near the village of El Hart in the foothills of Morocco's High Atlas Mountains. Here on the northwestern edge of the Sahara, villagers live in houses with high, thick mud walls built to keep out the desert heat. Drab and desolate in January, rose fields watered by the nearby M'goun River flower in late spring and supply a perfume industry in El Hart.

TOR EIGELAND

127

TOR EIGELAND (BOTH)

Zooming up and down the highway were huge trucks, pickups, four-wheel drives, and ordinary passenger cars. Roads or no roads, the automobile and the airplane are taking over desert transportation.

Soon we entered Tamanrasset, which lies near ancient Saharan trade routes. As early as 1000 B.C., when trade began to find its way from North Africa southward, horses and donkeys were used for the crossing. The camel, an animal ideally adapted to the desert, was introduced into Egypt around 250 B.C. By the third century A.D., camels had monopolized the caravan trade. By the end of the first millennium A.D., routes ran in a north-south direction, with a few winding east and west. They connected Moroccan and Tunisian cities with the Mali Empire, Timbuktu on the Niger River, and the oasis of Agadez. From Cairo traders traveled west and south to Gao and the Songhai Empire.

Romans had traded on the edge of the Sahara, but it was the Arab sweep of North Africa during the seventh century A.D. that enormously increased trans-Saharan commerce. Arab merchants and scholars established themselves in the black empires of the Sahel and West Africa. Arabic, spoken and written, became the principal language of commerce.

Salt, then as now, was a major trade item. Brought from Saharan salt deposits, it was traded for gold in the south. Also from the north and east came cowrie shells and military equipment, including horses. The cowries were used as currency. Horses were employed by black African kings for their cavalries. Gunpowder, glass beads, copper, textiles, jewelry, tools, books, and perfumes were also popular southbound goods. Luxury goods such as ivory, lion skins, leather, kola nuts, pepper, and even ostrich feathers went north from tropical Africa. Gold and slaves, however, were the commodities in greatest demand in the north. During the latter part of the Middle Ages, West Africa accounted for an estimated two-thirds of the world's gold production.

Peaks of prosperity in times of peace and slumps of economic hardship in times of political upheaval and war dominated caravan life. For the trader, survival was often a matter of paying his taxes, dues, or protection money to someone else. In the late 1600s, caravan trade entered an irreversible decline when ships of the sea began to replace camels—the ships of the desert.

A few camel caravans still wend their way across the desert, especially from the southern part of the Sahara into the Sahel. Camels laden with huge blocks of salt, dates, and millet plod between Taoudenni and Bilma in the north and Timbuktu in central Mali. In the eastern Sahara the semi-nomadic Beja still bring dromedaries through the desert from the Republic of the Sudan to Aswan in Upper Egypt. The camels are sold in Egyptian markets for transportation and for plowing—and for meat. Some years ago I waited to photograph one of these camel trains with Boris de Rachewiltz, who has studied the Beja. We were perched on a hill in the desert southeast of Aswan. The Beja, Boris believes, are descendants of a group that migrated from the Caucasus Mountains to Africa perhaps 6,000 years ago. Traveling between the Nile and the Red Sea, some Beja still carry crusader-type swords and still use daggers and primitive curved throwing sticks to protect themselves. Rudyard Kipling immortalized these people in his ballad "Fuzzy-Wuzzy," a term inspired by their impressive mops of hair, the original "Afros."

We waited for a long time. The sun rose higher. We were hot and thirsty. I looked off toward a tiny village far in the distance. A tiny white dot caught my eye. I focused on the figure through my telephoto lens. It was a man dressed in a white robe. He was approaching us, carrying something. As he came closer, I could see he was holding a tray. Balancing it, the man gingerly climbed the hill. As a sign of hospitality, the Egyptian villager had brought tea! Though lukewarm by now, never had a glass of sweet, strong tea tasted better.

Soon camels appeared on the horizon, as many as 90 of them. The animals seemed to be gliding just above the sand—an effect created by heat waves shimmering above the desert floor. Four Beja, proudly mounted on lead camels, guided their herd past us, never once looking our way.

Among the most famous traders of the Sahara are the Mozabites of the M'zab, an oasis region in northern Algeria. Extremely strict, conservative, and puritanical, they were considered heretical by many Moslems and were persecuted for centuries. In 1011, out of despair and for defense, they settled in the most barren, isolated area they could find.

Presently inhabited by some 100,000 people, the M'zab is the envy of the desert. An intricate and ingenious system of irrigation requiring immense amounts of hard work and discipline enabled the Mozabites to create a string of oases and, during the 11th century, to build a pentapolis of hilltop towns: el-Ateuf, Melika, Bou Noura, Beni Isguen, and Ghardaïa.

From their desert stronghold the Mozabites fanned out over North Africa, even into France, not as conquerors but as merchants. Their religious inner fire and money-making ability proved keenly compatible. The job of setting up grocery shops, selling cloth, carpets, spice, jewelry, and brassware, kept many Mozabite men away from their families and homes for years.

Judging by appearance, the rich Mozabites bear no resemblance to one's image of survivors of one of the earth's harshest climes. Many of the men, short, thickset, pale, round faced and black bearded, wear thick glasses and a little skullcap. The women, like ghosts, slip into and out of narrow alleyways and doors—unheard and just about unseen. And nearly unseeing. The women are covered from top to toe in white, loose-hanging garments. Only a tiny hole is left for either the left or the right eye to peer through.

A proud Mozabite guide, Cheriet Salah, made it possible for me to glimpse a small part of the closed, mysterious world of the Mozabites. We toured the food basket of the region, the man-made oases that lie in the valley between the five hillsides. Fed by wells and shaded by thousands of date palms, these well-kept gardens overflow with grapes, figs, tangerines, apples, apricots, and vegetables. Scented by orange blossoms, this cool, shaded world provides a refreshing contrast to the harsh desert outside.

Near the gardens, the five towns climb five hillsides. Crowned by minarets, their walls slanting inward to peak in fingerlike protrusions, the towns are a maze of narrow alleys, tunnel-like passages, and winding steps. With no cars or motorbikes allowed in most places, loaded donkeys clatter along, people squeezing against walls to make way.

My curiosity strained to find out what went on behind the city walls, especially in Beni Isguen. In this holiest of the M'zab towns, no stranger may spend the night, and the city gates are closed after dark—so tradition says.

Remnant of ancient marine life in the Sahara, a fossilized spiral shell called a goniatite becomes a collector's prize. People of the remote mountainous regions of eastern Morocco find rocks containing the fossils, chip them open, polish the exposed shell, and sell them at roadside stands and souvenir shops. Distant cousins of present-day chambered nautiluses, goniatites inhabited an ocean that covered much of the Sahara about 400 million years ago. Opposite: A Moroccan, clad in Western clothing and traditional turban, plies a family trade—polishing a goniatite with a hand-cranked tool.

"Is this true?" I asked Cheriet. He chuckled. "Did you see a hotel or a restaurant in Beni Isguen? There simply is no place to stay, no place to eat. But if you have friends in town, you can stay there. Things have changed. Nor do the gates close at night any longer." I wanted to enter a Mozabite house, but the M'zab is not a place where strangers are eagerly invited into a home. The houses face inward onto a private world that remained a mystery to me.

Where Beni Isguen is still medieval in character, Ghardaïa, capital of the sister cities, has moved into the 20th century, at least in appearance. Outside the ancient center of town, cars, trucks, buses, and people of every kind crowd the streets. The huge new Hotel Rostemides commands a sweeping hilltop view of the M'zab valley. Commercial jets service the local airport, and the Trans-Saharan highway comes right through here. Many people in the oil industry work nearby, and some factories are going up, perhaps signaling the end of isolation for the Mozabites.

I left Algeria and mapped out a journey into the desert of the Republic of Mauritania. Howling wind had been kicking up dust and sand for three weeks, and I almost literally blew into Chinguetti. This mud-and-brick oasis town in the northwest corner of Mauritania was once an important stop on the caravan trade route between Morocco and the Sahel. Chinguetti now ekes out a living from oasis agriculture, and from services it offers as a stopover point for desert nomads. The blowing dust and sand never ceased while I was in the oasis. A sandy wedge, a wadi about a quarter of a mile wide, separates the old and new districts. For nearly an hour I stood on a roof watching people trying to cross the dry riverbed. Stinging hot wind roared down the wadi and lashed the robed villagers as they stumbled across, half bent over, resembling bundles with the wrapping coming off in the strong wind.

Finally I straggled across, accompanied by Chinguetti's chief of police. He explained that the drought that was choking the country had reached disastrous proportions from 1969 to 1973. He took me to the town's biggest palm grove—once the pride of the village farmers. It was a sad sight. Sand had entered most of the gardens under the trees. More than half the palms had died in the drought, and the surviving trees at best looked unhealthy.

Sand filled the streets, and houses on the outskirts of the palm grove were half buried in it. Most of the ancient wooden doors had locks on them—people having fled. "There is very little water, so there is very little to eat, very little milk, very little meat," said the police chief. Drought has driven some of the people away, but most leave Chinguetti to look for jobs in the cities.

"Not only are the villagers leaving the villages, the nomads are leaving the desert," said Stanley N. Schrager, chief of the United States mission in Nouakchott, Mauritania's capital. The country, he explained, was experiencing one of the world's quickest population shifts. "Before the drought, two-thirds of the people were nomads and one-third urban," he said. "Now it is the other way around."

With drifting sands constantly invading Nouakchott, the nomads migrating to the city did not seem far from their desert home. Hundreds upon hundreds of their tents formed a poignant tapestry of contrast against the capital's gleaming villas and big new government buildings.

Delicate braids falling on the cheeks of a Fulani woman proclaim the infant she cradles as her firstborn (opposite). Many Fulani, a tribe of cattle herders, still roam from the Sahel to Senegal and into northern Cameroon. A village elder described the Fulani as "a race of eloquent rovers, unceasingly either about to arrive or about to leave, at the mercy of watering places or pastures." They indulge a fondness for ornamentation: bright clothes, shiny bracelets, and necklaces made of silver, cowrie shells, and beads. Recently faced with recurrent drought, many Fulani have settled in places such as the Inland Delta of the Niger River in Mali.

GEORG GERSTER

Through Nouakchott's dusty streets moved an exotic crowd: white Moors, black Moors, Arabs, Malians, Senegalese, a sprinkling of Europeans, mostly French, and the dark Haratins, who exist nearly everywhere in the desert. Traditionally, Haratins have given up a share of their agricultural produce to nomad masters in return for protection. But the master-serf relationship is slowly dissolving as the Haratins become increasingly independent.

I was swept along by bustling street throngs. Long, loose-hanging robes, mostly blue, and big turbans wrapped around the head and face dominated the male style. More colorful robes distinguished the women. In Mauritania, excessive plumpness equals female perfection and also indicates wealth. Many of the women were so overweight by Western standards they could barely wobble down the street. Resources for Mauritania's 1.4 million people are minimal. The subsistence-level agriculture has been dealt a terrible blow by the drought, and rich fishing grounds off the coast are still mostly exploited by foreign fleets. Mining of iron ore and copper, however, provides some foreign exchange, and trade takes place on the desert's edge, where pastoralists sell livestock and buy millet and cloth from sedentary peoples.

TOR EIGELAND

Persistent drought plagues the town of Chinguetti (left) and Nouakchott, capital of Mauritania (opposite). Through a haze of sand, residents of Chinguetti struggle across a dry riverbed. In 1981 rains sent water down this wadi for the first time in 20 years. Prosperous in the days of medieval caravan trade, the town now survives on crops of grain and dates. At Nouakchott, seif dunes border a mosque and vegetable plots at the edge of the city. Funded by the Canadian Red Cross, the gardens help feed nomads. When the disastrous drought of 1969-1973 killed off vegetation, desert dwellers who had once moved with the seasons settled in their tents near Nouakchott.

Leaving Nouakchott aboard a jetliner, I flew toward Casablanca. From there it was just a short hop to my home in Spain. But my mind parted ways with the plane and kept soaring over the Sahara. It swept back to the Red Sea coast of Sudan, where I had first seen the Beja, then inland to the Nile River, a winding thread through a desert canvas. I traveled downriver to huge, man-made Lake Nasser, which now teems with fish and crocodiles. I hovered over the ruins of ancient dynasties in the Nile Valley, then swept across Egypt's Western Desert, still partly unexplored.

Tunisia, Algeria, Morocco, Egypt, Mauritania, Mali, Niger, Chad . . . no longer just names on a map to me. I reflected on the ease with which my mind crossed these artificial borders, and I thought about the difficulties encountered by travelers in the Sahara who attempt to cross from one country to the next. To a large extent invisible political barriers have attempted to stop the natural flow of trade and people.

But empire builders and politicians come and go. The Sahara will soon forget them. And me. I do wish, however, that I could be granted a few more lifetimes and the freedom to explore the remaining mysteries of the world's mightiest desert.

GEORG GERSTER

Waffle pattern of earthen pans: An evaporation process extracts salt at Teguidda I-n-Tessoum, in western Niger. Workers pour a mixture of salt-laced mud into the large pans. After some of the water evaporates, the workers drain the residue into the smaller basins. Further evaporation concentrates the brine. At the final stage, workers scoop up the crystallized salt and shape it into bars. A Tuareg trader (below) arranges one-pound salt loaves, before packing them for transport.

FOLLOWING PAGES: *Heads held high above the blowing sand, camels carry salt across the Ténéré Desert in Niger. Tuareg caravaneers, once lords of trans-Saharan trade, today encounter border disputes and duties that restrict their journeys over ancient routes.*

DR. HANS RITTER (BOTH AND FOLLOWING PAGES)

DR. HANS RITTER (BOTH)

138

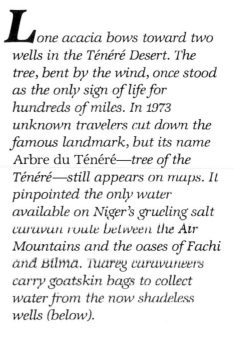

*Lone acacia bows toward two
wells in the Ténéré Desert. The
tree, bent by the wind, once stood
as the only sign of life for
hundreds of miles. In 1973
unknown travelers cut down the
famous landmark, but its name
Arbre du Ténéré—tree of the
Ténéré—still appears on maps. It
pinpointed the only water
available on Niger's grueling salt
caravan route between the Aïr
Mountains and the oases of Fachi
and Bilma. Tuareg caravaneers
carry goatskin bags to collect
water from the now shadeless
wells (below).*

THOMAS J. ABERCROMBIE, NATIONAL GEOGRAPHIC STAFF

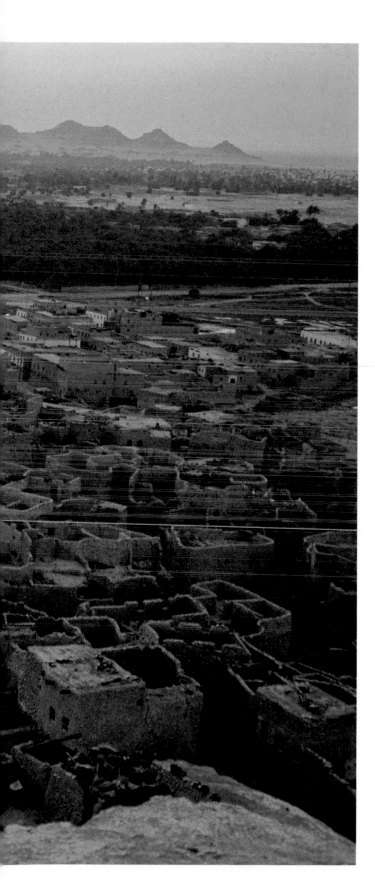

*W*alled rooftops of mud houses erode in the old quarter of Siwa, an oasis in northwestern Egypt (left). Heavy rains that strike every few years dissolve salt in the mud and cause the dwellings to disintegrate. Below: Black patches in a Landsat image reveal depressions where groundwater near the surface sustains Siwa. The edge of the Libyan Plateau, a rocky escarpment shaded brown, contrasts with the Great Sand Sea in the lower part of the image.

FOLLOWING PAGES: *The abrasive desert wind shapes a pillar of chalk near Egypt's Farafra Oasis.*

GEOPIC IMAGES/EARTH SATELLITE CORPORATION (ABOVE); GEORG GERSTER (FOLLOWING PAGES)

*I*n Egypt, a land 96 percent desert, a crew drills for water at El Harra, in the Bahariya Oasis (right). Men drilled for a month to a depth of 328 feet before hitting water. Below: Wasted water gushes from an uncapped well abandoned after a futile search for oil in the Qattara Depression. The water seeps underground, and where it surfaces vegetation grows. Opposite: Tongues of barchan dunes lap at irrigated farmlands in the Dakhla Oasis in Egypt's Western Desert. Competing with the desert, farmers have built stables on the edge of the dune in the foreground.

GEORG GERSTER (ALL)

GEORG GERSTER (ALL)

146

*A*dobe crown of buildings, Qara stands as the only town in the Qattara Depression area. Since the fourth century B.C., travelers crossing between the oases of Siwa and Bahariya have stopped here. Residents of Qara (far left) dry and sort dates, the town's main economic resource. Opposite: A nonpoisonous sand snake curls in a palm. The reptile feeds on rodents, lizards, and frogs that climb the trees to escape the blistering ground heat of the Sahara.

Sunny Plains and Misty Dunes

The Kalahari and the Namib of Southern Africa

By Joyce Stewart
Photographs by Georg Gerster

Morning sea fog moistens the dunes of the Namib, a desert on the Atlantic coast of southern Africa. Inland lies another major arid domain, the Kalahari Desert—home of the Bushmen, one of the few groups of hunter-gatherers still in existence today.

Moving soundlessly, three sepia-skinned Bushmen deftly pick their way across the thorny sandveld of southern Africa's Kalahari Desert. From a distance I watch as they track a hartebeest into the scrub. Perhaps other predators are stalking it as well—the lions I heard roaring just before dawn.

Suddenly Xhanabe, one of the hunters, vanishes. I scan the horizon for some sign of him. The other two hunters start chattering excitedly, their speech peppered with the clicks, fricatives, and glottal stops that punctuate the Bushmen's complex language. Then a slim brown arm shoots up through the golden grass. It's Xhanabe triumphantly holding aloft a huge moisture-laden tuber. Hunter has turned into gatherer!

Bushmen—also called San—are among the few remaining hunter-gatherers in the world. "About 60,000 Bushmen live in and around the Kalahari Desert," says Robert K. Hitchcock, an anthropologist who has worked among the San in Botswana. "No more than 5,000 still follow their traditional way of life, however, and by the end of the century probably none will be leading a purely hunting-gathering existence."

I had come to southern Africa to explore its deserts—the Namib as well as the Kalahari—and, I hoped, to meet these shy, gentle people who have managed not to conquer the desert but to live in harmony with it for thousands of years. It was November, and though scattered spring rain promised regeneration, drought still gripped this notorious "thirstland," where perishing from lack of water is an ever present possibility.

In the desert, I would discover, water—and the form it comes in: rainfall, fog, groundwater, floodwater—dictates the survival strategies of man and beast. It has shaped fantastic kinds of desert fauna and flora, and water has even helped shape the desert itself.

My journey began on the southeastern edge of the Kalahari. In Gaborone I visited Professor H. J. Cooke, head of the Department of Environmental Science at the University College of Botswana. "Lying athwart Botswana, the Kalahari stretches from the Zaire-Zambezi divide in the north to the Orange River in the south—a vast sand-covered plain occupying a gentle depression in the African plateau," he said. "Borne by wind and water, sand generated by weathering of the rocks of the surrounding uplands has been accumulating in this basin for probably five million years. Today the Kalahari sands—brick red, orange, rose, buff, gray, white—are more than 300 feet deep in places."

Lying in the southern part of this basin, the Kalahari Desert has oscillated between wetter and drier periods. As photographer Georg Gerster and I criss-crossed the desert, we saw evidence of climatic change everywhere. In the far southwest, burnished dunes encroach on once impressive rivers, now dry and choked with sand. One morning, against the shimmer of a desert dawn, I gazed transfixed as scores of silken-flanked springbok picked their way along a parched riverbed. The moving tide raised luminous clouds of dust that drifted and curled like golden fog rising from the phantom river.

Today the Kalahari is almost devoid of surface water—its main claim to desert fame. Although annual rainfall ranges from 4 to 30 inches or more, it is sporadic and localized. Yet as I traveled northwest from Gaborone, the deeper I went into the desert, the more verdant the landscape became. The greenness is

Ruling the central and western regions of southern Africa, the Kalahari and Namib Deserts occupy more than 166,000 square miles. The aridity of the Namib results mainly from the cold Benguela Current, which chills prevailing winds and inhibits their ability to create rain clouds. Less than an inch of rain falls annually in the central Namib; fog provides additional moisture— two or more inches a year along the Atlantic coast. Dunes, some rising more than a thousand feet, roll across much of the hyperarid Namib. The sand sea harbors scant vegetation and few birds or mammals, but a rich assortment of beetles, spiders, and lizards thrives in the dune ecosystem. To the east, wildlife roams the Kalahari, a vast sand-filled basin that supports varied grasses, shrubs, and trees. Despite scattered rainfall, almost no standing water exists in the Kalahari; the sand absorbs most of the moisture.

▬ *Hyperarid*	▫ *National Park or Game Reserve*
▬ *Arid*	⟶ *Prevailing Winds*
▬ *Semiarid*	

due to the sand. Wherever raindrops strike the thirsty earth, porous sand sucks the moisture down and stores it underground, where it's tapped by Kalahari flora. Wondrously adapted to the fickle environment, the grasses and trees can withstand long sieges of drought, and—like Xhunabe's prized find—huge tubers and roots hoard water against inevitable hard times.

The San too are wondrously adapted. Across the Kalahari, San organize their lives around water but follow a pattern adapted to local conditions. No source of water goes untapped. San extract liquid from the stomach contents of antelopes they kill. With grass tied to a stick they sponge up rainwater that collects in hollow trees. Some groups have no standing water available for as many as 300 days a year and obtain almost all their moisture from plants.

San in the northwestern Kalahari, however, enjoy several sources of standing water. During the dry season many of them congregate around natural seeps that they maintain as permanent pools. But as nearby food is depleted, these hunter-gatherers forage among the outlying dunes in the wet season.

During the brief summer rainy season, San of the central Kalahari cluster around hard-surfaced depressions called pans, which can hold water for a fortnight or more after a heavy downpour. But when the long dry season sets in, they must turn to other water sources. They scatter across the sandveld in small nomadic bands, searching for melons and tubers. These San obtain much of their moisture from gemsbok and tsama melons, eating up to ten pounds of melon pulp a day for a minimal liquid intake of three or four quarts.

Pushing toward the central Kalahari, I caught my breath when I spotted two small "haystacks"—the grass shelters that are home to the elusive San. Would they be occupied? Or would they be abandoned (Continued on page 154)

*C*hill dawn breaks over the Kalahari as Bushmen huddle in the warmth of a fire—both hearth and home to these hunter-gatherers (above). Bushmen usually sleep outdoors around small, smoldering fires; their huts provide shelter from summer rain squalls and fierce afternoon sun. Late in the day a family gathers around a cooking fire as sorghum simmers in an iron pot (opposite). They will roast the day's harvest of tubers and a clutch of young birds in the coals. This band of hunter-gatherers acquired its pots, pails, grain, and goats by trading antelope hides and doing odd jobs for farmers. Bushmen treasure children, showering them with love and affection. One of the women (far right) dotes on her niece, who wears a traditional fringed leather apron and beads.

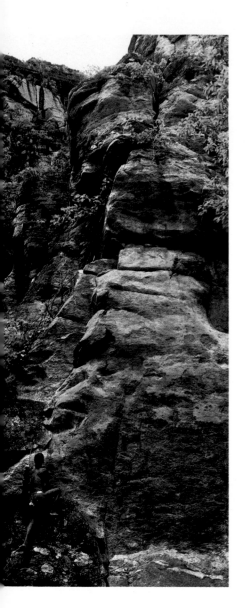

by these desert wanderers? As Georg and I approached, a wiry man wearing a leather loincloth came forward to greet us, his face creased in a welcoming smile. By an open fire his wife and daughter were plucking half a dozen birds for roasting, helped by three toddlers. Two older daughters had just returned from foraging. When we presented the customary gift of leaf tobacco, a toddler ran to fetch a pair of firesticks. Twirling one stick against another, his father, Xhanabe, ignited some dry grass. He lighted a pipe and passed it around—one puff each for me, Georg, and every member of the family.

Besides pipes, the San share many things: food, tools, tasks, pleasures. "Sharing is basic to the Bushmen's way of life," Alexander Colin Campbell, a noted San scholar, had told me in his office in the National Museum and Art Gallery in Gaborone. "In particular," he explained, "the Bushmen's elaborate system of sharing meat—everyone gets something—has traditionally ensured survival of the band, not just the successful hunter."

The hunter's reward is prestige—by hunting large animals a man proves himself a man. Traditional San rely on light bows and small poisoned arrows to kill game as big as elands and giraffes. Today hunting retains great symbolic significance, but as game has grown scarcer, it has decreased in importance in terms of subsistence. Gathering now provides up to 80 percent of the food of some San. They eat ostrich eggs, tortoises, and caterpillars, but for the most part they depend on a wide variety of plants for food and water.

In the Kalahari's far northwest, springs percolate through fissures in the Tsodilo Hills, a rugged mass of rock rising more than 1,200 feet above the dunes. These hills have been a haven for San and other wanderers for untold millennia. Climbing among the cliffs, I discovered haunting reminders of these desert sojourners—a legacy of some 2,000 paintings. Under overhangs and high on sheer rock faces parade elands, rhinoceroses, giraffes . . . usually rendered in red ocher and sometimes "signed" with a pair of red handprints.

"Gaining access to permanent water is one of the greatest dreams of all Bushmen," Bob Hitchcock had told me. Surely Tsodilo must have seemed a paradise to the San who camped there over the centuries. Its springs, however, can sustain very few people. But there is a modern answer to the Bushmen's dream—the borehole, a deep well.

"Though the water source may be new, the San's adaptability is not," emphasized Dr. John E. Yellen, an anthropologist I had met in Washington, D.C., before leaving for Africa. "The San have lived in the unpredictable Kalahari for at least 20,000 years," he said. "What has enabled them to survive is their ability to be flexible, to maintain and choose among a number of options. Those who excel at this, the San call 'masters of cleverness.'"

Settling by a borehole is one more option for these opportunists. But abandoning the nomadic life of hunter-gatherers for the sedentary life of herder-farmers may well mean abandoning many San traditions. Thus, though the San are not disappearing, their culture may be imperiled.

Sounding another alarm, Dr. Cooke warns: "By permitting the slow, insidious movement of more people and livestock into the Kalahari, boreholes pose a threat to the fragile desert environment."

The native vegetation can endure the natural vicissitudes of the Kalahari, including intermittent forays by migratory game. But the sandveld's blowing grasses cannot withstand the steady onslaught of cattle, sheep, and goats, which are making inroads into the green Kalahari. The desert's wildlife too is superbly adapted. Many species can go indefinitely without standing water, obtaining moisture from succulents, tubers, and dew-drenched grass. But, like the flora, the native fauna cannot contend against the increasing encroachment of humans and their herds.

Mobility means survival to the Kalahari's antelopes, which follow erratic rains across the veld, sometimes chasing a storm—and its promise of new grass—far beyond the horizon. Zebras and wildebeests make mass treks to seasonal feeding grounds. But fences have curtailed the free movement of these restless herds, and livestock is spreading into their age-old grazing areas.

Many of the migrants are drawn toward a sprawling complex of drying lakes, vestigial watercourses, and a vast inland delta that spills floodwater from the Angolan highlands over the sands of the Kalahari. In the east stretch the Makgadikgadi Pans, the shriveled remains of a Pleistocene lake that was once almost as big as Lake Victoria. To the south lies Lake Xau, shrinking and clogged with reeds. The slender umbilical that feeds it, the Boteti River, uncoils across the desert for more than 180 miles. In the west Lake Ngami fluctuates fitfully, filling up, then drying up completely, only to fill again.

All these fragile lifelines into the desert have their source in the Okavango Delta, a maze of papyrus swamps, serpentine channels, and flood-plains fanning out over 8,000 square miles of the northern Kalahari. Spasms of flood and ebb sweep over the delta, with the waters cresting at the height of the dry season. Coursing down from Angola, the Okavango River squanders its liquid treasure in the upper delta, where blue-black channels trace sinuous arabesques in an effort to snake their way through the papyrus swamps. Oozing, seeping, trickling, the waters of the Okavango breach the green ramparts and spill over the lower delta. Sparkling rivulets spin a silver filigree over grassy floodplains, circle palm-dotted islands, filter through thick beds of sedge, hug the wooded fringes of big sand ridges, and disappear in a mosaic of lustrous pools. At the base of the delta less than 4 percent of the intake emerges; the rest—a staggering 526 billion cubic feet of water annually—is lost through evaporation and transpiration, water loss from the surfaces of plants.

The permanent swamps of the upper delta harbor hippopotamuses, crocodiles, and rare aquatic antelopes. Where the waters retreat, however, other animals find haven. When the grass of the veld is sere, wildebeests and zebras surge into the delta, first onto the ridges and islands, then onto the floodplains as the water recedes. But when thunder heralds the summer rains, the plains animals scatter into the veld again.

Though fences have impeded the free-roaming herds, some conservationists maintain that fencing can also serve to protect wildlife in large reserves. Such a refuge exists in Namibia, at Etosha National Park, on the northwestern rim of the Kalahari basin. In all Namibia—apart from the rivers along its northern and southern frontiers—not a single perennial stream relieves the harsh aridity. At Etosha, however, subterranean water trapped in porous limestone feeds springs that once drew game from distant regions of south-western Africa. Today Etosha's wildlife finds (Continued on page 158)

Stylized giraffe evokes the skill of a prehistoric rock artist. Some 2,000 such paintings parade across the walls of the Tsodilo Hills in northwestern Botswana. Ancestors of today's Bushmen probably created most of the images, composed of a reddish pigment made of hematite, mixed with egg white, animal blood serum, or some other medium. Religious or aesthetic impulses, or the desire to record or ensure a successful hunt, may have inspired the rock paintings. Possibly following in the footholds of ancient artists, a Bushman (opposite) scales a cliff at Tsodilo. To his right, a gallery of rock art depicts rhinos and buffaloes, as well as giraffes.

*D*ivided world of the Namib: The Kuiseb River, the dark brown path cutting across this Landsat image, hinders a vast field of golden dunes from migrating northward with the wind across gravel plains. The Kuiseb curves more than 250 miles from its source in the highlands of Namibia to the Atlantic coast, where it sinks beneath a sandy delta, upper left. Giant linear dunes wrinkle the lower portion of the image; star dunes appear at lower right. Along the coast, transverse dunes ripple up to the delta of the Kuiseb, jump the river, and continue their march northward.

GEOPIC IMAGES/EARTH SATELLITE CORPORATION

but all ceased drinking and gave the lions a wide berth. Rump in the air, the lioness drank and drank, then went to the next pool and drank again. The cubs sampled every puddle in their path. As the lions ambled off, life at the water hole resumed its pace. Springbok locked horns and tussled, zebras squabbled, and 30 gangly ostriches flounced across the pan. At hundreds of Etosha springs the spectacle of the water hole plays daily during the winter dry season. But when the first summer rain falls, the herds leave the water holes and, like the plains animals in the Okavango Delta, vanish into the veld.

Continuing our quest, Georg and I traveled south, then westward over the Great Escarpment, where the African plateau tumbles down to the Namib Desert. Less than one hundred miles at its widest point, this narrow wind-whipped ribbon of rock and sand unfurls along the Atlantic coast for 1,300 miles, running from South Africa through Namibia and into Angola.

A land of pristine beauty, the Namib is also a land of contrasts. In the south, a coastal strip carpeted with succulents gives way to bare sand north of the Orange River. Gradually dunes build up into a sea of shifting crests and troughs that range from pale ivory on the coast to deep burnt orange inland to the east. Abruptly the dunes halt at the Kuiseb, a periodic river that arcs across the desert. In a startling metamorphosis, the Namib emerges north of the riverbed as flat, gray gravel plains rent by rock outcrops. The desert narrows along the Skeleton Coast, dune fields reappearing in the north.

Georg and I had been granted permission to visit the Namib Research Institute at Gobabeb, on the Kuiseb at the confluence of the Namib's three

major ecosystems: the southern sand dunes, the riverbed oasis, and the northern gravel plains. Rising out of the desert in this strategic bend of the river, the futuristic contours of the institute loomed like a welcome space station as Georg and I drove over the lunar landscape toward Gobabeb. We were greeted by Dr. Mary Seely, the enthusiastic director of the institute's Desert Ecological Research Unit.

With Mary we explored the region. The Kuiseb was verdant with acacia, fig, and tamarisk trees. Beyond the river towered coral-colored dunes. I was amazed to find traces of old watercourses running through the dune field. Back at the institute I learned about their origin. "Those scarp lines mark older courses of the Kuiseb," explained Dr. Nick Lancaster, a geographer studying dune formation. "The river has been pushed northward—probably under pressure from advancing dunes." So although seasonal flooding flushes sand from the Kuiseb, in the long run, rather than halting the dunes, the river may only be slowing their progress.

"According to my figures," said John Ward, a geologist who has been measuring dune movement, "the big dune at Gobabeb would take about 250 years to cross the river. In human time it may not be moving very fast, but in geological time it's galloping!"

Indeed, when I flew over the Namib, the desert seemed to be in motion. Cresting at heights of up to 450 feet, wave after wave of dunes rolls inland from

Granite bedrock bears the scars of weathering in the Namib. Below: Sliding tongue of sand inches a dune forward. Opposite: Deep in the Namib, a gemsbok roams some of the world's highest dunes at Sossusvlei.

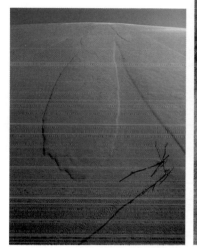

the sea, sweeping through a spectrum from ivory to apricot, caramel, even maroon. Plumes of sand trail off the crests, the wind resculpting the dunes grain by grain. Ripples scurry up a windward slope. A sandy tongue slides down a slipface. Big ridges spawn little ridges that skim the rims of craters. Star dunes link arms to form chains, or spiral off like pinwheels.

The largest dunes of the Namib rise in the center of the desert at Sossusvlei. This pan marks the end of an ephemeral river that cuts through the sand sea for 50 miles before its way is barred by dunes that soar more than a thousand feet above the valley floor. To explore these giants, Georg and I drove over a long, often tortuous route and entered the desert from the east.

Behind us loomed the purple battlements of the escarpment. Ahead stretched an austere gray floodplain. Low dunes gradually humped higher. Tentacles of sand glowed ocher, amber, dusty mauve in the late afternoon sun. A coppery fin shot out from the left. On the right, maroon sands spilled down from eroding sandstone terraces. Then before us rose the mighty dunes of Sossusvlei. Anchored on an armature of rock, they grow to awesome proportions. No rippling whimsy here, just pure structure—smooth, hard-edged planes, bold angular curves. The sands throb with color, both tender and intense—the roses of Picasso, the oranges of Gauguin.

Where did it all come from, the sand that fills the Namib with such spectacular sculpture? Most of it has traveled a long, circuitous route. The Orange River drains vast tracts of southern Africa's interior, discharging sand

and debris into the South Atlantic. Swept northward by currents, sand is washed ashore by the waves, then whisked inland by the wind.

The Orange has also brought down diamonds. Dislodged from volcanic pipes by erosion, diamonds mingled with gravel in ancient streams. This heavier debris was flushed to the sea in two great surges—first about 70 million years ago and again two million years ago—when the African plateau heaved and rose, turning tranquil rivers into raging torrents. Later the Atlantic flung its rich lode onto storm beaches, depositing diamond-bearing gravel on the coastal bedrock. Over the eons land and sea levels have fluctuated, so that today ancient beaches lie buried under billions of tons of sand in the Namib. Partly exposed fossil oyster beds in the dunes helped lead prospectors to these beaches and the richest trove of diamonds ever found.

Conventional mines yield about 70 percent industrial diamonds and only 30 percent gemstones, which—carat for carat—can bring a price thousands of times greater than industrials. In Namibia, however, the mining operations of CDM (Proprietary) Limited reap 95 percent gemstones near the mouth of the Orange. Across the estuary, South Africa's State Alluvial Diggings averages more than 96 percent gemstones. "In effect, the sea has presorted our diamonds," Donald Klopper, the assistant general manager of the mine, told me. "Only the best stones survive the journey to the coast and the pounding breakers of the Atlantic." Because of its fabulous riches, the Namib coast has been the focus of intensive study. Clues used in prospecting are now helping solve other mysteries as well. Fossils of warm-water oysters and similar evidence from deep-sea cores indicate that the cold Benguela Current does not date to the origin of the Atlantic. Hence neither does the present desert, for the Namib's extreme aridity is directly linked to this offshore current.

Rising in the South Atlantic and reinforced by the upwelling of frigid Antarctic water, the Benguela chills a wide swath of ocean northward into the tropics. The cold ocean in turn cools the sea breeze, limiting the air's capacity to take on moisture. A stable high-pressure cell forces dry air earthward, further inhibiting the buildup of rain clouds.

I was curious about the age of the Namib. "The present aridity probably didn't become severe until the beginning of the Pleistocene about a million years ago," Nick Lancaster told me at the Namib Research Institute. "But there have been wetter and drier periods. The Namib sandstone, from which some of the dark red sands in the east are derived, represents an earlier sand sea that probably dates back to the Tertiary, at least several million years ago."

"There's a fantastic amount of sand knocking around in the Namib, and a lot of it is definitely very old," John Ward added, "but the dunes you see are not necessarily old. More and more, in fact, geologists are tending to plumb toward a fairly young age for the present sand sea."

The Namib was once thought to be one of the oldest deserts on earth because of its rich native fauna, with so many species—mainly beetles, but spiders, scorpions, and reptiles, too—that live in waterless dunes, nearly devoid of vegetation. Nowhere else have comparable communities developed. Great age of the sand sea alone could not explain the Namib's distinctive fauna. "It's the result of a combination of factors," *(Continued on page 175)*

Moisture means life in the Namib: Dune grass collects water from fog (opposite). A tenebrionid beetle sips water from a droplet under its head (below). To gather moisture, the beetle climbs to a dune crest, lowers its head, and lets fog collect on its body. The beads of water roll down to its mouth. Bottom: A lizard found only in the Namib, Aporosaura anchietae *obtains its moisture from plants. Sharp jaw scales help the creature dive headlong into the sand to escape birds and snakes.*

ANTHONY BANNISTER (ALL)

Golden aurora envelops a herd of springbok roaming a dusty riverbed in the Kalahari Desert. Herds of migratory

game cross the sandveld in an endless quest for food and moisture.

*W*hite filigree of salt fringes small rain-filled depressions called pans in the northern region of Namibia's Etosha National Park. One of Africa's great game sanctuaries, the 8,600-square-mile refuge harbors such animals as elephants, cheetahs, and ostriches. Opposite: Thunderheads bring summer rains to the cracked floor of Etosha Pan. The dry lake covers more than 1,800 square miles in the heart of the park. Each year floodwaters and violent squalls turn the pan into a shallow lagoon. The murky water churns with catfish spawned by parents that survived the dry season by burrowing into the mud, living off body fat, and surfacing to use their auxiliary lunglike organs to obtain oxygen from the air.

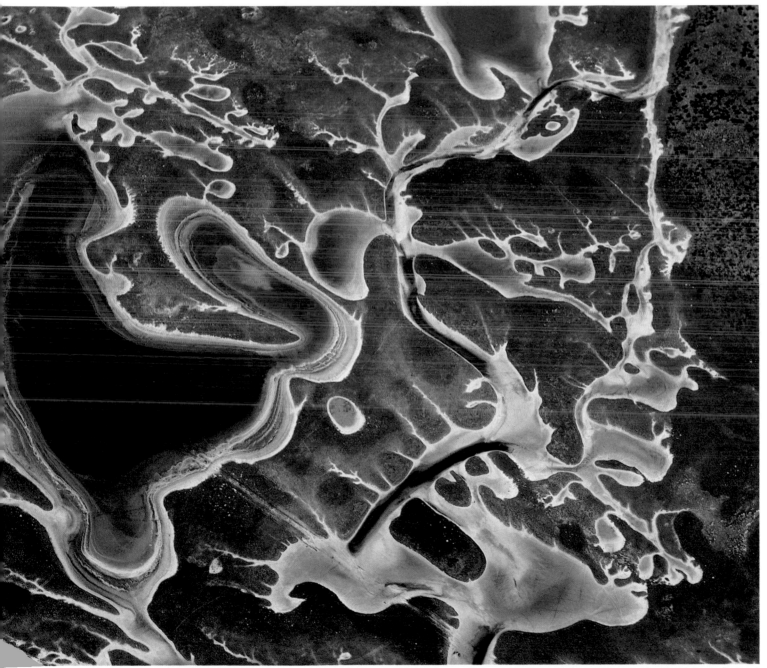

CAROL HUGHES/BRUCE COLEMAN LTD. (OPPOSITE)

*D*rawn together by thirst, gemsbok, springbok, and wildebeests share a permanent water source on the southwestern rim of Etosha Pan. Shallow pools form when rainwater that has collected underground in porous limestone beds seeps out onto the pan's clay floor. Left: Elephants loll in a deep artesian spring south of Etosha Pan. Floating reeds and decaying leaves add to the sour odor of the mineral-rich water. A thirsty elephant can consume more than 45 gallons from the spring in a single drinking session. Far left: A secretary bird takes off to search the Etosha area for rodents, insects, and snakes. The long-legged predator kills by stamping its prey with both feet.

*S*wampy waterways of the Okavango Delta fan out over the northern Kalahari. A channel struggles through papyrus beds in the upper delta (left). On the left lie green perennial swamps; on the right, vegetation on higher ground turns brown as seasonal floodwaters ebb. An African jacana darts across a lagoon spangled with water lilies (right and far right). In the lower delta, game trails radiate from a palm-dotted island that formed around an old termite mound (below).

170

M*aze of dunelike islands breaks up the salt-encrusted floor of the Makgadikgadi Pans, part of an ancient lake bed in the northern Kalahari. The pans cover an area bigger than Maryland and Delaware combined. The islands formed from large accumulations of windblown sand during a drier period. Slight differences in vegetation mark subtle contour lines created by fluctuations in water level. Great herds of wildebeests and zebras etch dark trails in the alkaline clay floor of the pans. The animals wander from island to island to graze on the fresh grasses that sprout when summer rains come.*

172

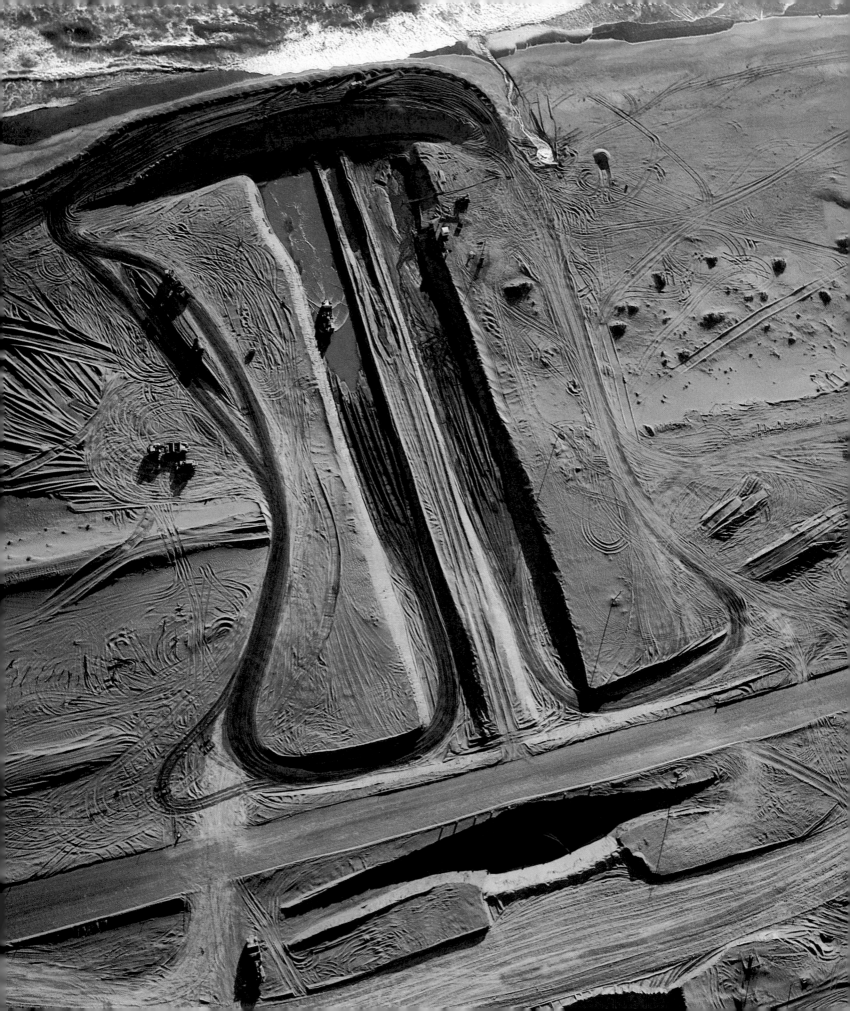

Mary Seely told me. "Earlier species—already adapted to a dry though not yet hyperarid environment—gave an evolutionary head start to the present species. Also, the extent of the Namib dunes has excluded many predators, permitting the proliferation of species that are for the most part conspicuous, flightless, and without defenses. Lastly, the cool coastal climate with frequent fog provides crucial moisture for life in the Namib."

Conditions that cause the Namib's aridity also, paradoxically, create its life-sustaining fog. When humid air from far out in the Atlantic is drawn over the Benguela Current and suddenly cooled, the moisture condenses to form fog. Light winds carry the fog inland, sometimes 50 miles or more.

At Gobabeb, precipitation from fog—about an inch a year—usually exceeds rainfall. On the average, a dripping fog rolls in every ten days or so, providing a reliable source of moisture for the dune inhabitants. Rainfall, though, is highly irregular. Nevertheless, rare heavy rains—often years apart—permit grasses to germinate and flourish briefly. When these plants die, their dried remains can last for years in the desert climate, providing a fairly dependable food base for many small Namib animals.

On warm windy afternoons when gusts lash the dune crests, rustling eddies circulate the plant particles over the bare slopes. Then, long legged beetles go skittering over the sand at astonishing speed in pursuit of their windblown dinner. On cold foggy mornings, however, these beetles move slowly but deliberately when they emerge from the sand to drink. The "fog-basking" beetle climbs up to a dune crest, faces into the wind, then does a headstand by lowering its front end and raising its rear end. Fog striking the beetle's back forms water droplets that run down to its mouth.

Fog also nourishes strange and marvelous plants in the Namib, the most extraordinary being *Welwitschia mirabilis*. This botanical wonder starts out with two narrow leaves emerging from a carrotlike base. As the plant grows, the base expands, and the same two leathery leaves keep on growing and growing—splitting as they grow wider, coiling and fraying as they grow longer—for hundreds, even thousands of years. One scientist has calculated that the leaves produced by a monster *Welwitschia* over its 2,000 year lifetime could carpet a track three yards wide and 400 yards long.

The rich variety of life forms harbored in the harsh extremes of the Namib seems only to grow more fantastic the more hostile the environment. But in my journey of discovery I had learned that even this hyperarid corner of the world is, like the Kalahari, not hostile but nurturing to those who know its secrets. Bleak, forbidding, alien—none of these. The wide-horizoned deserts of southern Africa are part and parcel of our vibrant, vital earth—home of incredibly creative life, source of endless wonder and overpowering beauty.

All these faces of the desert came together on my last flight over the Namib when I saw a dripping, drenching fog from the air. What a beautiful, exhilarating sight! Rolling in over the dunes, the fog foamed thickly in the troughs—roily gray, blue, even dusky violet. Surging up the slopes, fog filled the hollows along the ridges; swirling, swelling, then billowing over the crests, it cascaded down the slipfaces. Thus milked by row after row of ruddy dunes, the fog surrendered the moisture that sustains the miraculous life of the desert.

Digging for diamonds on the coast of the Namib, earth-moving machines expose layers of gravel for sampling (opposite). A high seawall holds back the rush of the Atlantic. The coastline of the Namib contains the world's highest known concentration of gemstones. Below: Laborers dislodge diamonds from bedrock. Gemstones, weighing from two to four carats each, glitter in a sorter's palm (bottom).

FRED WARD/BLACK STAR (TOP)

Drifting sand buries memories of an elegant past in Kolmanskop, an abandoned diamond-mining town in the Namib near the Atlantic Ocean. In 1908 a workman removing sand from the local railway line found diamonds, the first glint of gems in this desert. Miners recovered almost five million carats from Namib mines over the next six years. The deposits played out by the end of the 1930s, and Kolmanskop residents abandoned their stylish homes. The handpainted Art Deco pattern on the tattered wall of a dining room (above) hints at the town's onetime opulence.

FOLLOWING PAGES: *Ship of the desert, the* Shawnee *lies awash in a sand sea on the coast of the Namib. Shifting sands along the shoreline, often shrouded in fog and lashed by storms, snared the vessel during a night passage in 1976.*

176

*S*harp eyes and an intimate knowledge of their environment help Bushmen find plant foods, the mainstay of their diet. These foragers exploit more than one hundred species of plants in the Kalahari. In the dry season only a shriveled stem among the tangled grasses may betray an edible root or bulb. Summer rains bring leafy greens and sweet-fleshed berries. Beans and nuts supply protein. Delicacies include Kalahari truffles and monkey oranges, gathered by throwing a well-aimed stick (far right). A young boy uses a twig to fork out the tangy pulp of the succulent fruit (opposite).

*T*emporary bounty, rainwater from storms like the one brewing on the horizon
may last for six weeks in this pan in the Khutse Game Reserve (above). As Bushmen
scoop water into ostrich eggshells (opposite), a baby sleeps soundly in his mother's
kaross, a leather cloak that doubles as a carrying bag. The mother will nurse her
baby for almost four years; during that time she may carry the child nearly 5,000
miles as she gathers food, visits friends, and changes campsites.

Winds of Change in Ancient Realms

The Middle East

By Tor Eigeland

World's largest body of sand, the desolate Rub al-Khali echoes its Arabic name, "the Empty Quarter." The desert countries of the Middle East produce an ocean of oil. Nearly 50 years of petroleum operations have brought wealth, power, and change to the lands of ancient Arabia.

E. G. FRIESEN/BRUCE COLEMAN INC.

Up ahead the full moon hanging above a red sand dune in a pink, clear sky looked like a silver ball about to roll down a hill. An exquisite sight. But it was shattered by the roar of the powerful tractor-trailer rig that was straining to haul its heavy load of drilling gear up the dune.

We were deep in the Rub al-Khali, the formidable Empty Quarter of southern Arabia. This sand sea lies on the Tropic of Cancer, in the same arid belt that has created the Sahara. The Empty Quarter, where some dunes soar higher than 800 feet, covers about 250,000 square miles, the largest expanse of sand in the world. It could accommodate France, Belgium, and the Netherlands with room to spare. On the most difficult leg of our journey, we were headed for a drilling site more than 600 miles from Dhahran, the Persian Gulf headquarters of Aramco—the Arabian American Oil Company now owned by Saudi Arabia.

The mighty diesel engine growled and snorted in protest as the rig's balloonlike tires sank into the soft sand. "*Bi-Allah*, this is a bad one," groaned the Bedouin driver. Slowly, we inched upward. Finally, the chugging rig cleared the top of the dune. We shot down the other side at a hair-raising speed and stopped in a wide trough between two gigantic dunes. Our 13-vehicle supply convoy would park here for the night.

The Bedouin slaughtered two sheep and prepared the traditional fare of rice and mutton. An enormous tray with a mound of steaming rice and meat was placed on a carpet on the sand. I joined the drivers, who squatted in a brotherly circle to eat in the manner of their Bedouin ancestors: left knee on the ground, the other raised, the right hand serving as the eating utensil.

Having enjoyed Bedouin hospitality many times in the course of covering the Middle East for 20 years as a photographer and a writer, I had become adept at some of the ways and manners of these desert dwellers. At least I no longer spilled rice all over the carpet.

In the Empty Quarter I found Aramco exploration crews working around the clock, pushing miles of pipe armed with drill bits deep beneath the desert's surface. Hundreds of millions of years ago organic matter was deposited on the floor of an ocean that ebbed and flowed over today's Arabian Peninsula. Eons of decomposition and pressure formed the once living material into sedimentary layers of liquid and gaseous hydrocarbons—oil and natural gas that make up some of the world's largest known petroleum reserves.

For days the only signs of life I had seen in the Empty Quarter, other than the drilling crews, were a few lizards, one viper, and two black-masked women of Al-murrah, a Bedouin tribe. Of all the peoples of the world, few have mastered living in the desert better than the Bedouin. These original Arabs have little use for national borders. The stock herders will roam as far as 1,200 miles in any direction to find pasture and water for their sheep, goats, and camels.

The Bedouin personify strong traits forged by the desert: endurance, an uncompromising faith, a strong loyalty to their tribe, and a rather poetic soul. Centuries in the desert have taught them skills for surviving in places where most people cannot. To snare scarce meat, the Bedouin perfected the use of falcons and the Saluki, a speedy hunting dog of the greyhound family. Above all, it is the camel that has enabled the Bedouin to survive in the desert. Besides providing transportation, this hardy beast gives milk, sometimes the only food and drink available in these water-scarce lands.

Degrees of dryness break the Middle Eastern deserts into three major areas. Rugged mountains rise at the edge of the hyperarid zone on the Arabian Peninsula's western coastal plain. In the south and southeast sectors of Arabia, the Rub al-Khali smothers a region the size of Texas. Arid areas include high rocky plateaus and sweeping sand seas. Semiarid climate prevails in Arabia's northern mountains, where summers inflict long droughts, and cool winters bring rains and flooding.

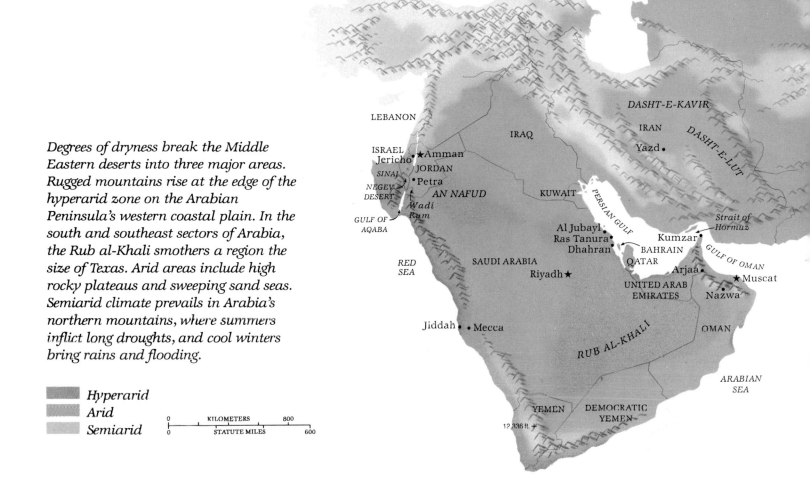

- ▨ Hyperarid
- ▨ Arid
- ▨ Semiarid

KILOMETERS
0 — 800
STATUTE MILES
0 — 600

I had dreaded that milk. Years earlier, before embarking on my first desert exploration trip, I had been told in Dhahran that I would have to live mostly on camel's milk, rice, and dates. The thought of warm, foamy milk spiced with camel hair and sand and drunk from a communal bowl dismayed me.

The dreaded moment came in the tent of Mussaud bin Muhammad Al-murri. Mussaud, a tribesman of Al-murrah, was camping in the Empty Quarter southwest of Dhahran. During the evening, after my first meal with him, he said: "I don't think I am boasting when I say that my camels have the sweetest milk in the world." A big frothy bowl was brought to me. "Drink!" commanded Mussaud with a knowing smile. "Drink!" My throat tightened. I put the bowl to my lips and quickly drank some of the warm froth, trying not to taste the milk. Then it happened. I tasted it . . . and loved it. The sweetest milk I had ever had. Mussaud could not have been more pleased.

At this moment my driver, Corbi, arrived to pick me up, and I experienced a typical Bedouin greeting. Corbi and Mussaud first kissed each other's noses gently, then spoke something like:

"*Ahlan wa-sahlan*—You are welcome."

"*As-salām 'alaykum*—Peace be upon you."

"*Wa 'alaykum as salām wa rahmat Allah wa barakatu!*—On you peace and the mercy of Allah and his blessings!"

"How is your health?" "Good. Allah be praised." "May God protect you." "May God give you safety." "How are you?" "Good. Allah be praised." "How is the herd?" "Allah be praised, good. And to *(Continued on page 192)*

*S*ons of the desert, Bedouin gather for a majlis (below)—an informal audience with a member of Saudi Arabia's royal family. The right of speaking man-to-man with one's leaders lies rooted in ancient tribal practices. Bedouin customs and conservative Islamic beliefs remain the basic tenets of Saudi society. Islam's holy text, the Koran serves as the nation's constitution, as well as the framework for economic policy and social mores. Five times a day, faithful Muslims—like the two at opposite, lower—kneel toward Mecca and pray. Modern innovations, such as a portable TV set in a nomad's tent (opposite), sometimes contrast sharply with traditional Saudi life.

ROBERT AZZI/WOODFIN CAMP & ASSOCIATES (ALL)

FOLLOWING PAGES: *Devout pilgrims crowd the Sacred Mosque at Mecca in Saudi Arabia, birthplace of the Prophet Muhammad. In a swirl of motion, newly arrived worshipers circle seven times around the draped Kaaba—the most sacred shrine of Islam.*

MEHMET BIBER (FOLLOWING PAGES)

you good." "How is the old man?" "Good. May God protect you." "God give you peace and a long life." "May God give you a long life." After these formalities, Mussaud said: "What is your news?" And a conversation about camels, grazing, people, and weather followed. I was to hear variations of this litany often.

For centuries the Bedouin successfully put the desert frontier between themselves and the outside world. Then, in 1933, King Abdulaziz Al Saud, who had united rival tribes and cities to create the Kingdom of Saudi Arabia, reached an exploration agreement with the Standard Oil Company of California. Foreign influences in the form of oil exploration machinery and operators of such technology began moving into the land. In 1938 Americans struck oil in the area of Dhahran.

By the end of 1981 some ten million barrels of oil a day, about 25 percent of the world's total production, were gliding out of the Persian Gulf aboard low-riding tankers. The race to recover and market rich reserves of oil and gas has upped energy stakes worldwide and has made the entire Middle East jittery, turning it into a corner of conflict where volatile alliances shift like the sands. From Syria, Israel, Iraq, and Iran in the north to the Yemens in the south, everyone is directly or indirectly involved in a mad patchwork of struggles. Turmoils range from fratricidal ones to clashes between Arabs and Israelis. Like the Bedouin who are no longer inviolate in the desert, Saudi Arabia may never be quite the same after the Sacred Mosque at Mecca was seized by Muslim fanatics in November 1979 and then liberated only after a bloody battle. A month later, the Soviet invasion of predominately Islamic Afghanistan set off shock waves throughout the Middle East and the world.

Petroleum wealth has also had a jarring effect on conservative Islamic Arabian society—desert and city dwellers alike. The abundant flow of money has stimulated Saudi Arabia, as well as other Persian Gulf states, to develop at an accelerated pace. Flying by helicopter from Dhahran north along the gulf coast one hot August day, I looked down on what I remembered as small towns, clean desert, and oases. But now parts of the landscape had turned into a vast construction site with all its accompanying litter. A huge new industrial city is being built almost from scratch at the site of the once charming fishing village of Al Jubayl. More than one million foreign workers have been imported to help the Saudis meet their ambitious modernization program. Giant jets daily disgorge industrialists and salesmen who have opened the region to a flood of consumer goods. New schools and universities are springing up, and many young people study abroad with full financial support from their governments. National education for girls—instituted only about 20 years ago—means they now fill the classroom; many enter the universities as well.

With the boom have come problems. Some women leave the halls of higher education only to come up against a Saudi custom decreeing that they cannot take a job where they are in contact with men. Easy money, luxuries, and the availability of good jobs in the cities have made many farmers abandon their fields. Growers of dates, formerly an important staple, face a shrinking demand as new riches bring new tastes. Saudi Arabia at the beginning of the 1980s was importing about 70 percent of its food. First used to cater to the growing

Wilderness of tan and blue wrinkles part of the Rub al-Khali in this Landsat image of the desert's northern reaches in the United Arab Emirates (opposite). Dots of clouds—a rarity here—float above rippling fingers of sand in the upper left corner. Horns of crescent dunes, in the lower half of the image, point in the wind's northwesterly direction. Dry wadis show up in shades of blue. White indicates either light-colored sand or dried salt.

GEOPIC IMAGES/EARTH SATELLITE CORPORATION

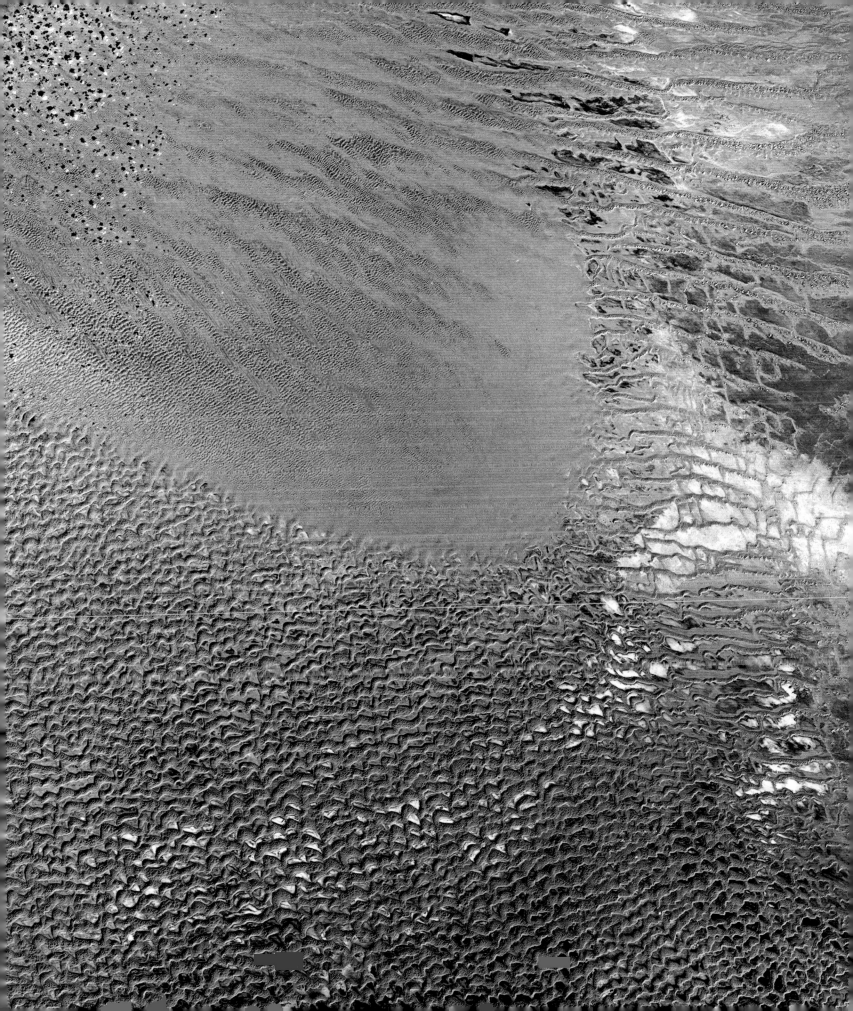

MEHMET BIBER (BOTH)

numbers of foreigners, imported foods are now increasingly consumed by the Saudis themselves, who number more than six million. Many Saudi supermarkets carry Australian beef, American coffee cakes, and Danish butter cookies—alongside packaged camel meat.

Connected with the booming growth is a concern over the water supply. Saudi Arabia is a country with few permanently flowing rivers. Efficient pumps may be drawing out groundwater faster than it can be replaced. New desalinization plants help meet the increasing needs of more people who require more water for construction, for agriculture, and for the home.

Nearly overwhelmed by Saudi Arabia's urban explosion, I began to yearn for the romantic Arabia of the past. I found a part of it in the Sultanate of Oman, a land of watchtowers and castles, and a thousand miles of unspoiled beaches along the Gulf of Oman and the Arabian Sea.

Temperatures as high as 130°F make Oman one of the world's hottest countries. Against the nation's backdrop of mountain, sea, and desert live a people with storybook grace. Wearing brightly fashioned turbans, many Omani men dress in the elegant *dishdasha*—long, white, flowing robes with a wide belt made of silver thread. In the middle of the belt, at front, hangs the *khanjar*, a curved ceremonial dagger, an elaborate work of art with a hilt and a scabbard of gold or silver.

Rolling out the red carpet, Saudi officials prepare a welcome for Queen Elizabeth II of England at Dhahran airport (opposite). Saudi Arabia's international influence has grown dramatically since Abdulaziz Al Saud united rival desert tribes to form a kingdom in 1932. Six years later the country's first commercial oil well began producing; it still flows at the rate of 1,600 barrels a day. An average Saudi well today produces 12,000 barrels of oil daily. Lavish earnings from petroleum production have brought jetports and highways to this land once linked by camel routes. Right: White-robed King Khalid with his brothers, Crown Prince Fahd on the right and Prince Abdullah on the left, tours a seawater desalinization plant in Jiddah. The facility turns 20 million gallons of brine a day into fresh water for the growing city.

As striking as the men are, it was the Omani women God copied to make the rainbow. Slender and graceful, the women love brilliant colors. Nearly all wear trousers with a dress or tunic covering the torso. Most cover their heads with shawls, and some still wear a veil to keep from being seen by men. Many Omani women, however, have shed the veil and have taken their place in today's work world. Women serve in the Omani police force, and even the Sultan's air force boasts one female pilot.

Open for all to see is the modern face of Oman: gleaming buildings, good hotels, desalinization plants, and excellent, well-marked roads. The major force behind Omani progress is His Majesty Sultan Qaboos bin Said. In 1970 Sultan Qaboos deposed his father, Sultan Said bin Taimur, who had kept Oman in medieval isolation. At the time of Taimur's overthrow the Sultanate had six miles of asphalt road, running from the Sultan's palace in Muscat to the airstrip in Ruwi. Nine years later there were 292 miles of roads. In the first decade of Qaboos's reign the number of schools grew from 16 to 363. For the first time, Omani girls attended school. Prior to 1970 only one hospital and 13 doctors served a country of more than one million people. By the close of 1981, hospitals numbered 14 and more than 200 doctors cared for the Omanis.

I arrived in the country just after the ten-year anniversary of Sultan Qaboos's takeover. "Hopes are high that in the near   *(Continued on page 202)*

LYNN ABERCROMBIE (ABOVE)   THOMAS J. ABERCROMBIE, NATIONAL GEOGRAPHIC STAFF (ABOVE AND BELOW)

*O*il tankers gather off a newly built town near Muscat, Oman's capital. At this safe berth near the mouth of the Persian Gulf, ships wait as long as possible before slipping into the gulf and making their run to oil ports in war-troubled waters. About one-quarter of the world's petroleum comes from the Arabian Peninsula. Huge refineries, such as the one at Ras Tannurah (left), in Saudi Arabia, extract gasoline, diesel fuel, and other products from crude oil. Oman's proven petroleum reserves could fall below a profitable level after the year 2000. Since 1970, therefore, the nation has used profits from petroleum to diversify its economy. Seeking alternative resources in Oman, workers drill for core samples at Arjaa, site of copper mining 4,000 years ago in Mesopotamian times (far left).

TOR EIGELAND (BELOW AND RIGHT)

THOMAS J. ABERCROMBIE, NATIONAL GEOGRAPHIC STAFF (BELOW)

*S*unset surf of the Arabian Sea spills a golden shimmer onto a beach in southwestern Oman. Fishermen have pulled rich catches, including mackerel and sardines, from these waters for centuries. Opposite: At Kumzar on the Strait of Hormuz a fisherman repairs nets, and at Muscat Harbor (far left) villagers ready hand-hewn dhows equipped with outboard motors. Oman offers subsidies to fishermen in the hope of turning the country's traditional fishing livelihood into a profitable export industry.

future our country will be a source for agricultural products for all the gulf area," His Excellency Hassan Abdullah al-Murrassa, undersecretary of the Ministry of Agriculture, told me.

Most farming takes place in Al Batinah, a 200-mile-long stretch of land lying between the Al Hajar Mountains and the northeast coast. Farm crops consist mainly of dates, limes, alfalfa, mangoes, and vegetables. In the south, where a more temperate monsoon climate prevails along the coast, tropical fruits include papaya, coconuts, and bananas.

While highly automated agribusiness methods are being introduced in Oman and in the other gulf states, the Omani government has recruited foreign engineers and crews to pump new life into a long-neglected, ancient water distribution system called *aflaj*. This Arabic word is the collective term for all the water channels that make up an irrigation system, a single channel being a *falaj*. The lifelines of Oman, the aflaj tap water sources in nearby mountains and in aquifers. The largest volume of water in the system comes from underground. To reach an aquifer, the Omanis sink a well, then dig subterranean channels that siphon the water. The downhill slope of each falaj forces water down the mountain grade along the floor of a tunnel that leads to surface canals near villages and fields.

Another underground resource vital to Oman is petroleum. Oil wells in the country's deserts produced 333,000 barrels daily in 1981 and enriched the

LYNN ABERCROMBIE (ABOVE AND PRECEDING PAGES)

Agricultural link with the past, a canal carries water to date palms harvested by an Omani farmer in the oasis town of Nazwa (left). Oman's high-quality dates—prized as far away as India—remain the country's principal export crop. Water from distant mountains follows a man-made network of subterranean conduits leading to surface canals that wind through oases and villages. After residents divert water for drinking and for household use, farmers receive allotted shares to irrigate their crops. On an experimental farm at Suhār (opposite), diesel-powered pumps draw well water, and rotating sprinklers shower circular fields of fodder crops and vegetables.

PRECEDING PAGES: *Cultivated terraces stairstep the slopes of Al Jabal Al Akhdar—the Green Mountain—in northern Oman. Springs and annual rainfall averaging 12 inches nourish these plots of onions, garlic, and fodder crops.*

nation's economy by more than four million dollars a day. Oman's limited oil reserves, however, are just a drop in the barrel compared with the extensive reserves in other gulf states. Bracing for the day when its petroleum pools fall below a profitable level, Oman is diversifying its economy. The country emphasizes traditional means of livelihood, such as fishing and farming. The government today pays for new boats and equipment in an effort to lure back more than half of Oman's fishermen who gave up the sea for higher-paying jobs in the construction and oil industries.

Relying on ancient desert methods in modern times is a practice also followed by the Hashemite Kingdom of Jordan. Here, about 2,000 miles northwest of Oman, the famous Royal Jordanian Desert Police ride camels to patrol the nation's dry sector, which envelops all but one-fifth of the country.

The nation's desert police corps was started in 1930 by a British major, John Bagot Glubb (Glubb Pasha). He acted on orders from Prince Abdullah of Transjordan, who wanted to end tribal feuding. Glubb Pasha selected recruits from the sons and relatives of rival *badw* chiefs. From the term *badw*, Arabic for "desert dwellers," comes the word "Bedouin." Shrewdly, Glubb Pasha clad members of the new force in uniforms that appealed to Bedouin pride: the checkered red-and-white *kaffiyeh*, or headcloth; the *kumbaz*, a long kiltlike garment with a wide belt; and crossed bandoliers. Bedouin still make up 80 percent of this elite corps, and with good reason—no one knows the desert as well as they do. *(Continued on page 207)*

TOR EIGELAND

*S*heer splendor of Wadi Rum beckons riders of the Royal Jordanian Desert Police, an elite Bedouin force that patrols the country's desert, roughly 28,000 square miles. A patrolman scans for smugglers (upper right). In Amman, Jordan's capital, bandoliered troopers brace for weekly inspection (far right). An officer helps a nomad repair a water pump at a desert well (opposite).

TOR EIGELAND (ALL)

In Amman, Jordan's capital, I called on the chief of the desert police, Lt. Col. Anbar Dahash. "We help anyone who may be in trouble. Get a sick Bedouin to a hospital, fix a broken water pump at a desert well. One of our main functions along the borders is to prevent smuggling—from Jordan into the neighboring countries and vice versa. Cigarettes, television sets, electrical appliances come from Saudi Arabia and go to Jordan and Syria. And alcohol is smuggled to Saudi Arabia, where it is completely illegal."

Patrolmen were once mounted solely on camels, but times are changing. "About 30 camels are used for patrol duty today in mountainous and hilly terrain where vehicles cannot enter," the colonel told me. "The majority of the work is done by vehicles equipped with two-way radios. Some are pickups with mounted machine guns. Our 36 desert police posts all have radios as well, with new microwave communications being installed. A whole search operation can actually be directed right from my office."

A desk phone rang, interrupting Colonel Dahash. When he hung up, he was obviously pleased. He announced that one of his patrols had just apprehended a truck that had crossed illegally from Saudi Arabia with 45 television sets. "We had to chase them and there was gunfire. My men shot out the tires of the truck and stopped them," he said.

Bedouin love a chase. Less than 24 hours after leaving Colonel Dahash, I found myself bouncing in the front seat of a speeding pickup with a police sergeant and a driver. Two policemen were in the back, holding on tight to a mounted machine gun for support. We were 90 miles east of Amman, near the Saudi border, rocketing over the flat, but bumpy desert. We were in pursuit of a red pickup racing ahead of us in a dust cloud. It was heading straight north toward the border with Syria, and it seemed to be pulling away from us. Picking up speed, we flew over the sand.

I glanced at the speedometer—and wished I hadn't. We were clipping along at nearly one hundred miles an hour. But now we were gaining. We drew alongside the pickup. The policemen, waving guns, brought the truck to a stop. Dust plumes from both vehicles washed over us like a gritty wave.

The red doors of the pickup flew open and out jumped two Bedouin. Grinning, they greeted us politely. They were both Saudi tribesmen. Their papers and the contents of their truck were examined. They carried blankets and water only. Why had they been driving so fast? They laughed uproariously. "Fast?" they said. "We love to drive fast!"

The police sergeant later explained to me that the two had crossed the border from Saudi Arabia to join their families. As there had been more rain in Jordan this year, many Bedouin had come across from Saudi Arabia with their herds to graze in Jordan for the summer. Jordan allows them to do this with little more formality than checking in at the nearest border post.

I was on patrol again a few days later. This time with Abdullah Faraj, commander of the two-towered desert police garrison at Wadi Rum in southern Jordan. About 5:30 in the morning, after a great deal of commotion—saddling camels and singing loudly—we rode out of the fort and ventured deeper into Wadi Rum. Its overpowering silence enveloped us. The hot sun was climbing fast, spotlighting scenery stunningly beautiful. Dome-shaped and

TOR EIGELAND (BOTH)

Keyhole image of another age awaits visitors at the end of the dark, narrow chasm that leads to Petra, a hidden city nearly 2,000 years old in southwest Jordan. Nomads known as Nabateans built Petra by enlarging natural grottoes and by chiseling elaborate stonework facades inside a rock-walled valley. The Pharaoh's Treasury (above) probably served as a royal mausoleum. Other tombs cut from sandstone cliffs perch atop caves (opposite). Using Petra as their stronghold, the Nabateans dominated the caravan trade and ruled a rich empire.

Making the desert bloom: Rows of plastic warm soil and help melon seeds germinate in Israel's Negev Desert (opposite), a region of cold winter nights, little rain, and salty groundwater. Melons also grow in greenhouse soil (below) heated by underground pipes that draw hot water from geothermal pools. Possible new crop for Israel, the jojoba (bottom) tolerates alkaline soil and yields a high-grade liquid wax valuable for pharmaceutical and industrial use.

TOR EIGELAND (ALL)

craggy rocks, varying in color from yellowish gray to pale copper to black, seemed sculpted by an extraterrestrial genius. Once a broad river two miles wide, Wadi Rum now harbors a river of sand between parallel walls of rock. The opposing granite cliffs of Jebel Um'Ishrin and Jebel Rum rise in magnificent splendor above the valley floor.

The wadi was created during a geological age when a gigantic shrug of the earth forced up granite and red sandstone mountains and enormous blocks of craggy rocks. Today the dark-stained stones are worn smooth by time and wind. Pink, brown, and near-white sand dunes lap up against the majestic outcroppings. No wonder the more spectacular scenes in the movie *Lawrence of Arabia* were filmed here. Indeed, Lawrence himself (T. E. Lawrence, a British liaison officer) and Arab leader Sharif Husein ibn Ali rode out of Wadi Rum in 1917 to direct Bedouin raids against Turkish troops during World War I.

For three days we roamed the historic dry riverbed. At dusk we would make camp. The Bedouin love to tell stories, recite poetry, laugh, and sing. The last night in the field, Commander Faraj was in especially good form. Each tale was for my benefit and each began with Faraj speaking my name in Arabic.

"*Abu Ra'd*—Father of Thunder?"

"Yes, Abdullah."

"I want to tell you something. If you sleep in the desert at night the hyena will come. He will come, walk around you, measuring you. Then he will dig a hole in the ground as long as you. He will dig down—deep, deep, deep—and suddenly he will push you in and start eating you!"

Each story was followed by hilarious laughter. Finally the policemen fell asleep on their blankets in the sand. Early the next morning, I sleepily checked myself over. No hyena had tried to eat me. But as I was having my first glass of sweet tea in the growing daylight, one of the policemen suddenly laughed and pointed to strange zigzag marks in the sand. We leaped up and found that all around us were the fresh tracks of deadly vipers.

Tracks of a different kind led me into another Bedouin world some 45 miles north of Wadi Rum. Hoofprints of horses carrying visitors mark the trail that winds through a narrow 300-foot-deep chasm of red-stone walls called the Siq. Suddenly the path ends at a fissure that forms the gate of Petra, the hidden ancient city of the Nabateans. First mentioned as nomadic tribesmen in the seventh century B.C., the Nabateans literally carved a capital for themselves out of rock. On a small plain inside a canyon of sandstone cliffs, they built elaborate temples and buildings of rose-colored stone. Monumental tombs, some with facades 120 feet high, were cut into the walls of nearly every cliff.

The Nabatean empire thrived on aggressive commerce. Petra stood on the overland trade routes that crossed from Madain Salah in Saudi Arabia north to Damascus in Syria. The Nabateans monopolized the caravan spice trade. They ran their own camel trains and guided and protected foreign caravans, charging duty on the goods that passed through their domain. Romans annexed Petra in A.D. 106, but the city continued to prosper until around A.D. 400, when it became a quiet outpost of the Eastern Roman Empire. Desert nomads gradually moved into the city.

Today some Bedouin live permanently in Petra, still drawing water from centuries-old cisterns chiseled *(Continued on page 212)*

*W*orld's oldest town, tree-shaded Jericho flanks the Wadi Qilt, which curls out of the rumpled Mountains of Judah. Since farmers started growing crops more than 10,000 years ago, people have lived here beside Elisha's Well. The biblical spring gushes forth a thousand gallons of water a minute. Almost continuously, people have fought over this vital water supply. Archaeologists have discovered remains of defense towers dating from 8000 B.C. Today other conflicts trouble this land. Beyond the wadi near the mountains, an abandoned Palestinian refugee camp spreads out on the Israeli-occupied West Bank.

GEORG GERSTER

211

TOR EIGELAND (BOTH)

New generation of Bedouin, boys of the Shararat tribe in Jordan fill oil drums with water for their goats and sheep. Opposite: Future herdsman or college graduate? This lad may have a choice. Free schooling and job openings tempt the Bedouin to trade the freedom of the desert for the settled life of the cities and towns.

out of stone by the Nabateans. Masters of irrigation, the Nabateans hardly wasted a drop of water. Catchment basins were hewn out of rock, and natural basins were dammed up to collect water. At the top of cliffs channels were carved to lead the water to the basins. Trees were planted nearby the basins to shade them and to slow evaporation. Around their farmlands, the Nabateans built stone fences that caught rainwater and channeled it to terraced fields.

A stone's throw from Petra and across a political chasm live a modern-day people who, I found, have become as expert as the Nabateans at making the most of limited resources. With vigor and imagination the Israelis are developing methods of irrigating crops in the Negev, a rocky, mountainous, desert tableland that forms more than half of Israel's territory. I was eager to learn how the Israelis are solving water problems in their efforts to turn parts of the Negev into productive land.

Dov Pasternak, head of the Division of Desert Agriculture of Ben Gurion University's Institute for Applied Research, told me: "In Israel we're using practically all our fresh water, above ground and underground. We cannot significantly increase our supply of fresh water. We try to tackle this problem within three different categories. Number one is to increase water-use efficiency; two, to increase crop yield per unit of water applied; and three, to use alternative sources of water.

"We achieve water-use efficiency in several ways, such as employing drip irrigation. This system trickles water through thin plastic pipes. Holes in the pipes deliver to each plant in a row a measured amount of water. As for using alternative sources of water, we have runoff water, sewage water, and brackish groundwater. Also dry-land fodder crops have been introduced. By testing hundreds of fodder plants of desert origin, we have culled two excellent species that can flourish in the Negev: Australian saltbush and four-wing saltbush from the United States."

Outside Pasternak's office hangs a sign: "I'm a jojoba nut!" This promising species, first reported on by the University of Arizona in 1933, is a bushy Sonoran Desert plant valuable to Israel because it can grow in arid land. Its bean, when processed, yields a high-grade liquid wax. Similar to sperm-whale oil, the product has numerous industrial uses for lubrication and for manufacturing pharmaceuticals and cosmetics.

"The jojoba is being studied worldwide now. At this institute we recognized the potential of jojoba in the 1960s," Pasternak said. "Since then we have developed high-yielding varieties. Today in the Negev we have planted 270 acres of jojoba. The central Negev is a huge area—the biggest area available for development in Israel.

"But until three years ago there were only three settlements here," Pasternak said. "We couldn't expand any farther because there was no more water. Now, because of our research on ways to use brackish water, we have been able to renew the settling of the Negev. Israel plans to extend settlements all the way to the Gulf of Aqaba and to increase the Negev population to a million people in the next 20 years."

As I ended my travels through the deserts of the Middle East, my mind was crowded with the images of the changes I had seen. Especially vivid was the contrast of past-and-present life-styles of the Bedouin. TV antennas sprout above the goat-hair tents of the nomads, and shiny pickup trucks may be parked outside. Tire inner tubes and oil drums are used to carry water. Bedouin sit at the wheels of 25-ton trailer trucks rather than on the lead camel in caravans. An increasing number of Bedouin are moving into towns and cities as the 20th century unrelentingly penetrates deeper into the desert. In some areas, such as the Negev, space is simply running out for the nomadic way of life—a matter of bitter dispute.

The whirlwind of change in the Middle East brought to my mind the words of Rashid ibn Henzab, a white-bearded Al-murrah poet, who had told me: "We who live with the camels and their sweet milk are at peace with the universe. Those people who go to the cities or drill for oil are no longer true Arabs. This oil will become unimportant, and those who leave the desert won't know how to survive in the place from where they came."

Survival in the desert has always been a struggle for the Bedouin. For thousands of years, seasonal changes have challenged and shaped the existence of these nomads. They have met the challenge by moving from place to place in search of food and water for their herds and flocks. Their survival has depended on their ability to be flexible in the face of hardship and change.

But never before have these wanderers experienced changes as abrupt as those of the last 20 years. Whether modernization will make the Bedouin grow soft and lose their ability to endure despite change remains an open question. Ironically, comfort could be the greatest challenge these tough-minded desert people have ever faced.

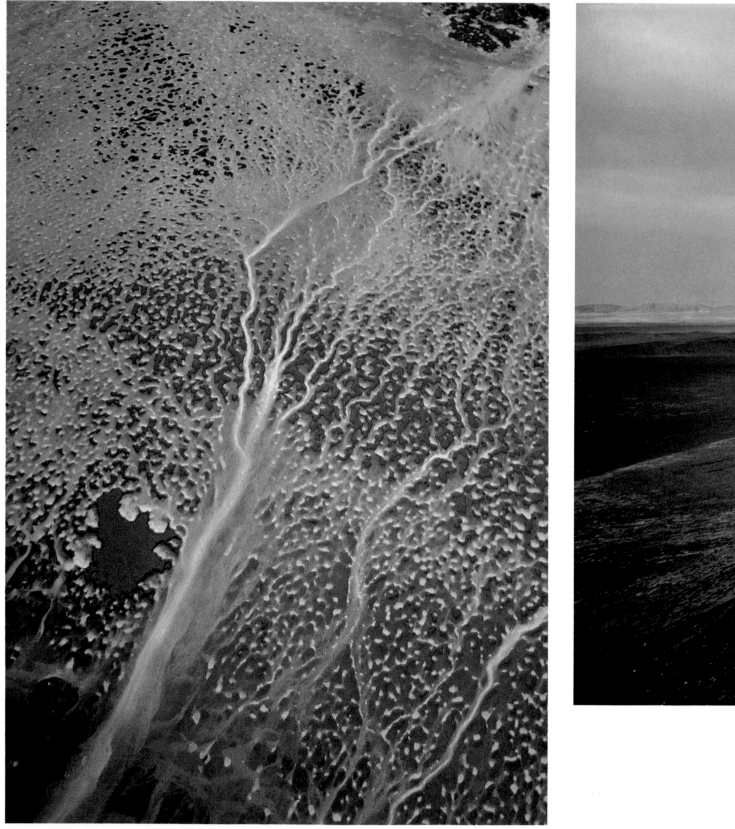

NATIONAL GEOGRAPHIC PHOTOGRAPHER JAMES P. BLAIR

*I*ntricate drainage pattern reveals the branches of runoff from a rare rainstorm in the Dasht-e Kavir, the world's largest salt desert (opposite). The 200-mile-long tilted playa blankets part of northwestern Iran. Thousands of years of evaporation produced the salt deposits. In Iran's Dasht-e Lut—Sand Desert— salt whitewashes a volcanic outcrop (above).

NATIONAL GEOGRAPHIC PHOTOGRAPHER JAMES P. BLAIR

GEORG GERSTER (BELOW AND OPPOSITE)

*M*anholes in the desert
(opposite) mark shafts that lead to
underground aqueducts in Iran.
The tunnel galleries tap water in
aquifers and efficiently transport it
to villages. Workers clear silt from
an older channel (left). Laborers
dig a new access shaft (above). The
ancient irrigation system, called
qanats in Iran and aflaj in Oman,
shields water from the desert
sun, thus reducing loss of water
by evaporation.

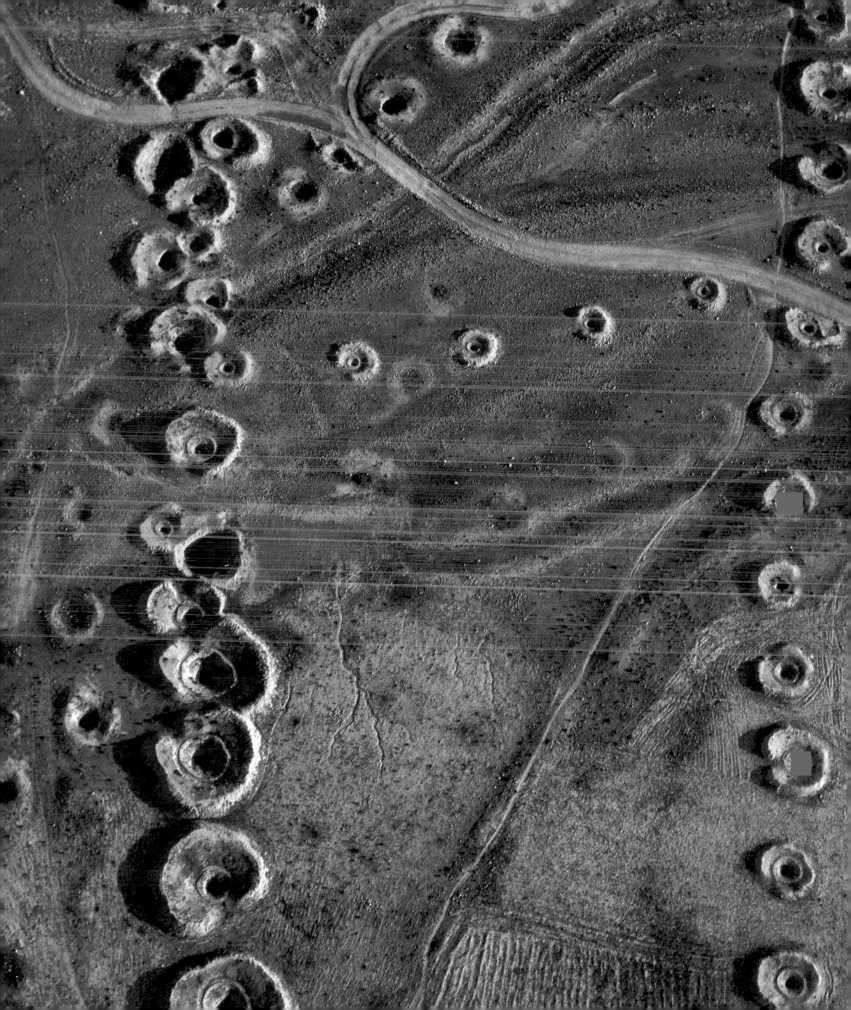

Fabled Deserts of the Orient

The Taklimakan and Gobi of Asia

By Dr. Farouk El-Baz

Silent sentinel, a mud-brick beacon overlooks Yin Shan gorge in western China. Fires kindled atop these twin spires warned of invasion in the borderlands during the Han Dynasty (206 B.C. to A.D. 220). Rulers coveted this desert region for East-West trade routes known as the Silk Road.

JIN BOHONG

218

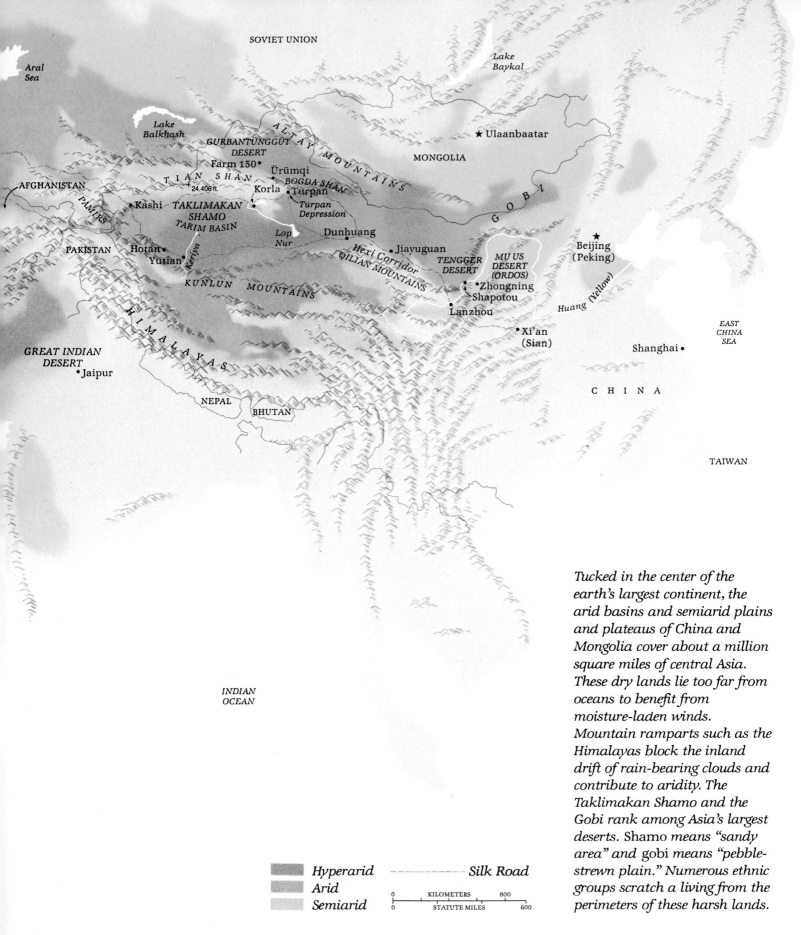

SOVIET UNION

Aral
Sea

Lake
Baykal

Lake
Balkhash

★ Ulaanbaatar

GURBANTÜNGGÜT
DESERT

Farm 150•

ALTAY MOUNTAINS

MONGOLIA

AFGHANISTAN

TIAN SHAN

Ürümqi

BOGDA SHAN

24,406 ft.

Korla

Turpan

GOBI

•Kashi

PAMIRS

TAKLIMAKAN
SHAMO

Turpan
Depression

TARIM BASIN

Lop
Nur

Dunhuang

★
Beijing
(Peking)

PAKISTAN

•Hotan

Kerya

Yutian•

Jiayuguan

Hexi Corridor

•Zhongning

QILIAN MOUNTAINS

TENGGER
DESERT

MU US
DESERT
(ORDOS)

Shapotou

EAST
CHINA
SEA

KUNLUN MOUNTAINS

Lanzhou

Huang (Yellow)

GREAT INDIAN
DESERT

HIMALAYAS

•Xi'an
(Sian)

•Jaipur

Shanghai •

C H I N A

NEPAL

BHUTAN

TAIWAN

INDIAN
OCEAN

Tucked in the center of the
earth's largest continent, the
arid basins and semiarid plains
and plateaus of China and
Mongolia cover about a million
square miles of central Asia.
These dry lands lie too far from
oceans to benefit from
moisture-laden winds.
Mountain ramparts such as the
Himalayas block the inland
drift of rain-bearing clouds and
contribute to aridity. The
Taklimakan Shamo and the
Gobi rank among Asia's largest
deserts. Shamo means "sandy
area" and gobi means "pebble-
strewn plain." Numerous ethnic
groups scratch a living from the
perimeters of these harsh lands.

Hyperarid

— — — — — Silk Road

Arid

Semiarid

0   KILOMETERS   800
0   STATUTE MILES   600

220

"I wish we had time to study the Gobi Desert," I said, looking out the window of the Beijing-Lanzhou train.

"You too! I really thought that *you* would know better. 'Gobi Desert'—there is no such place-name," said Dr. Zhao Songqiao.

My host knew that his statement was perplexing. Dr. Zhao, professor of physical geography at the Academy of Sciences' Institute of Geography in the People's Republic of China, smiled. "In China," he said, "we call *any* desert 'gobi' if it is pebbly, and 'shamo' if it is sandy. As we go west, you will see many gobi plains."

In all the geography courses I had taken, in all the books on China I had read, and in many of the maps I had seen, the term "Gobi Desert" had designated the northern part of China and the adjacent plains and semiarid steppe of the Mongolian People's Republic. The term appears in some of the early accounts of expeditions into this area. Explorers must have used "gobi"—a Mongolian word that describes a type of terrain—as a place-name.

"If 'Gobi Desert' is a misnomer, it is commonly used throughout the Western world," I said. "It should be corrected."

"Yes, I agree," Dr. Zhao said. "We hope it will be corrected."

I directed my attention to the maps we had unfolded in our train compartment. I shifted closer to the light, a lamp with a ruffled cloth shade. Outside, the late-summer twilight was rapidly fading behind the dark green mountains moving past our window. It had been morning when we boarded the train in Beijing (Peking), the capital of China. The coal-burning train was rumbling westward into the heart of this Asian nation of a billion people, the most populous country in the world.

I was in China as a member of a scientific delegation of desert specialists sponsored by the National Geographic Society and China's Academy of Sciences. We had come to study parts of China's arid lands and, particularly, to observe how the Chinese have tamed the desert.

In the soft glow of our compartment I studied the maps, concentrating on China's arid and semiarid areas, which total 505,000 square miles. The dryness of China's interior basically stems from the terrain's great distance from the world's oceans. Furthermore, towering mountain ranges shield the country's wastelands from moisture-laden winds. The Altay Mountains to the north prevent rain clouds from reaching the Gurbantünggüt Desert, which fills the center of the Junggar Basin in China's northwest corner. Similarly, the Himalayas, rising to 29,000 feet in the south, shelter the largest vegetation-free sand sea in China—the Taklimakan Desert, which covers about 130,000 square miles in the country's far west.

The arid Gobi is a sequence of gravelly plains and small depressions in northern China and the Mongolian People's Republic. Bordering this area are semiarid steppes where sand and shallow brown soil spotted with grasses blanket the plains. Between this bleak landscape and the Taklimakan Desert lie several smaller arid areas, including the sandy deserts of Mu Us, Ulan Buh, Tengger, and Badain Jaran.

The train lurched as we jostled around a curve. I looked up from the maps. "These maps don't show gobi plains. Where will we see them?" Dr. Zhao answered, "In many places. We will see some on the way to Dunhuang in Gansu

and in several places in Xinjiang (Sinkiang). But tomorrow we will see the loess lands of the Yellow River."

The term "loess"—from the German word meaning "loose"—denotes an unstratified deposit of fine-grained soil. In northern China such deposits of yellow silt mantle more than 200,000 square miles, one of the largest accumulations of silt in the world. The loess deposits stretch into the basin of the Yellow River—so named because of the buff yellow color of the soil that saturates the river water. Our train crossed miles of loess, which varies in thickness from a few feet to 300 feet. Where did it all come from?

It was the work of the wind, which in Pleistocene times probably stripped the Mongolian Plateau of its fine-grained silt and deposited load upon load of the particles in northern China. Years of wind erosion have left the Mongolian Plateau nearly bald of topsoil. Thus the "gobi" was formed. Pebbles and cobblestones—too large for the wind to carry away—speckle the surface. From this austere area the Mongols sprang to force an empire upon much of the world in the 13th century.

The loess carried to China as a gift of the wind has been put to good use by the Chinese. Today farmers irrigate the silty plains with water from the Yellow River and its tributaries. Wheat, bean, and mustard fields cover most of the countryside. Crop yields run high because the silt contains vital nutrients. In this regard the region resembles parts of the central plains of the United States, where fertile loess—blown in from northern areas—projects a finger as far south as Mississippi.

Our express made a sharp turn southward and followed the Yellow River. The loess land began to grow drier. Suddenly we saw in the distance the imposing silhouette of the Great Wall. During the Qin Dynasty in the third century B.C., the emperor who unified China linked existing defense walls and built what is now known as the Great Wall of China. The wall winds across about 2,000 miles of China's rugged land. It served to keep out the raiding nomadic predecessors of the Mongols. Subsequently many segments were built by other dynasties.

Between the cities of Zhongning and Zhongwei the Yellow River separates the fertile fields along its southern banks from the lifeless dunes of the Tengger Desert to the north. As we rolled into the Tengger, large sand dunes moved closer to the railroad bed. At Zhongwei we disembarked to visit a place named Shapotou, which means "at the head of a sandy slope." The name describes the location, the edge of the Tengger, a shamo where dunes creep along the foothills of the Xiangshan, an east-west mountain range.

In 1956 the Beijing government wanted to connect the railroad of eastern China to the line in western China. But one small segment west of Zhongwei presented a major problem. The Xiangshan was earthquake prone. It could not be trusted to support the railbed. Just north of the mountains were the shifting dunes of the Tengger. Earthquakes could not be checked, but could the motion of the dunes be halted?

This question has been asked by inhabitants of all the sandy deserts of the world. A popular approach to solving the problem has been to put trees in the path of the dunes. In the Sahara of North Africa, oasis dwellers plant tamarisk

JIN BOHONG (ALL)

Hewn from a hillside near Dunhuang (opposite), hundreds of grotto-shrines fulfill a monk's vision: "a thousand Buddhas in a cloud of glory." During the fourth to fourteenth centuries, monks living in the Caves of the Thousand Buddhas thrived on patronage from pilgrims traveling to India and back along the Silk Road. The dry air of western China preserves murals decorating a temple at Baicheng (above). A Buddha endures the centuries in the shrine near Dunhuang (top).

trees and date palms. The trees serve as a barrier. The system works for a while, but as the dunes grow, they engulf the trees.

In Algeria, Morocco, and Tunisia eucalyptus trees are used as windbreaks rather than as physical barriers. Growing in thickets, the scrubby varieties of desert eucalyptus catch sand blown by the wind. Although the trees limit the movement of sand, they do not completely prevent it.

Some desert peoples, such as those of southern Peru and the Indians of North America, have experimented in anchoring sand dunes with pebbles and cobblestones. This method, like the others, has its flaws. Some of the sand migrates past the pebbles and accumulates as dunes downwind.

In oil-rich countries such as Iran and Saudi Arabia sand dunes are sprayed with petroleum to form a protective, wind-resistant layer. Oasis dwellers in Egypt build fences of dried palm fronds atop crests of migrating dunes. In the Great Indian Desert rows of hay barriers are erected atop the dunes. But neither the fronds nor the hay completely stabilize the sand.

In China, officials have adopted a successful method of dune control. The strategy involves laying out straw barriers in a checkerboard pattern instead of arranging the straw in parallel rows. This method was used to solve the problem at Shapotou.

"Over a period of two years," said Zhu Zhenda, director of the Lanzhou Institute of Desert Research, "it probably took as many as 100,000 labor-days to do the job."

Laborers jammed thatch in a grid pattern over an area of sand some 25 miles long and 1,600 feet wide. The squares of straw, each about 3 by 3 feet, follow the contours of the dunes. This ingenious treatment confines the movement of the sand within the straw squares.

"It looks like a giant fishnet laid upon the dunes," I said to Professor Zhu as we inspected the site. He pointed out grasses and drought-tolerant shrubs growing on either side of the railroad track. "The vegetation forms a barrier that also helps stop dunes from drifting across the rails," he said. Occasionally, strong storms sweep sand onto the railbed, and people must sweep the track clear. But the railbed has been free of dunes ever since the rail link between eastern and western China was completed in 1958.

From Shapotou we went to Lanzhou, an industrial city of two million people on the Yellow River. Centuries ago, Lanzhou served as a major stop on the Silk Road, one of the oldest trade routes between the Orient and Europe. Ancient chroniclers of China, including Ptolemy, described the treacherous route by which merchants transported valuable commodities—gold, jewels, spices, and silk. In time the route came to be known to Westerners as the Silk Road.

Reeling silk from the cocoon of the silkworm began in China possibly as early as 3000 B.C. The Chinese managed to keep the secrets of the silk process from outsiders for thousands of years. Silk fabrics exported to the Middle East, Greece, and Rome brought the Chinese a handsome profit. Raw silk was allowed to leave China, but death was the penalty for exporting silkworm eggs.

The oasis towns along the Silk Road became wealthy trading centers. What saved the oases were permanent sources of   *(Continued on page 230)*

Threads of Eastern cultures mingle at Kashi (opposite), where a Uygur rug merchant examines a carpet displaying motifs from Persia and the Caucasus. Once a stop on the Silk Road, Kashi now exists as a Chinese border city near the Soviet Union. Indian and Middle Eastern influences and remote desert location have produced a freedom-loving people here. China holds a firm grip on the region but has developed the commune system slowly, allowing more liberties than permitted farther east. After meeting their commune quota, Kashi merchants—as they have done for centuries—sell goods in a "free market," one not controlled by the government.

JIN BOHONG

*F*ertile fields lined by poplars surround ancient ruins near the Turpan Depression, at minus 505 feet the lowest point in China. Snowmelt from the Tian Shan— Celestial Mountains—feeds some area streams, such as the one Uygur women ford on their way to market (opposite). The region of hot days and cold nights produces melons and white seedless grapes renowned for their quality (far right). The heat of summer days increases the fruit's sugar content. The variation in daily temperatures prompts a local saying: "Wear a fur coat in the morning but a cotton shirt at noon, and in the evening eat melons around a fire."

NATIONAL GEOGRAPHIC PHOTOGRAPHER BRUCE DALE (ALL)

*O*ctober snows stipple the shoulders of the Tian Shan, a towering range crossing the top of this Landsat image (right). Tracings of meltwater fan out in white; the runoff ultimately nourishes agricultural patches, in red, at the edge of the Turpan Depression. A large sand sea appears as a dark oval on the right. Below: China's forbidding interior challenges a truck convoy near Turpan. Bottom: A traditional Uygur donkey cart, modified with bicycle wheels and carrying fodder for sheep, rolls past the ruins of Gaochang. The city served as the capital of a Uygur state for many centuries.

NATIONAL GEOGRAPHIC PHOTOGRAPHER BRUCE DALE (BOTH, ABOVE); GEOPIC IMAGES/EARTH SATELLITE CORPORATION (OPPOSITE)

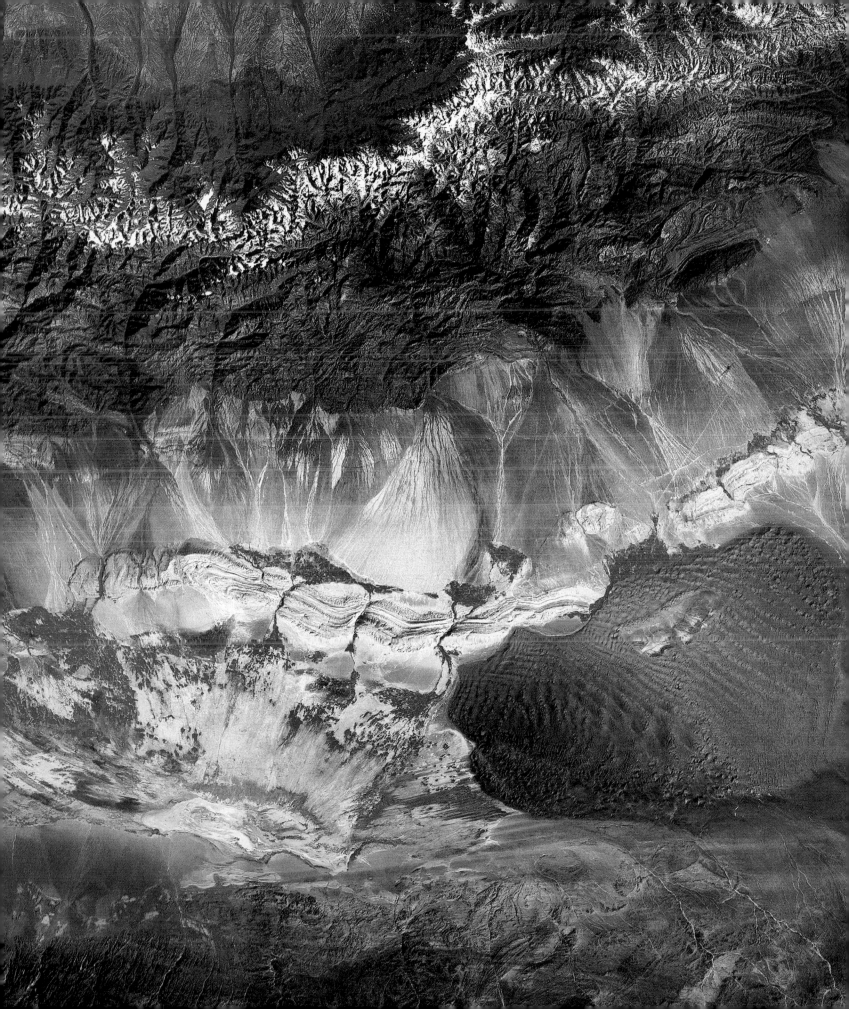

water, mostly rivers flowing from nearby mountains. On the southern edge of the Taklimakan, many rivers dried up or switched courses—forcing abandonment of the towns. Some oasis towns here were covered by shifting dunes thousands of years ago.

The central part of the Silk Road comprised many routes, all of which were basically caravan trails. Merchants going west always approached the rugged desert and mountain portion of the trip by traveling through the Hexi Corridor in Gansu. West of Jiayuguan at least three alternate routes beckoned. The map on page 220 shows the two principal trails—one winding south and one trending north of the Taklimakan—coming together at Kashi. Here the westward-moving merchant faced another choice of routes through the windy and icy passes of the cloud-scraping Pamirs.

Our train shadowed the Silk Road toward Yumen. The track snaked through the Hexi Corridor, a narrow passage skirting the hills north of the majestic Qilian Mountains, whose highest peaks soar more than 15,000 feet.

Oases in the Hexi Corridor blossomed with vegetation. Bright yellow mustard fields emblazoned terraced hillsides where cattle grazed. Hay bundled in conical heaps on the slopes announced the grain harvest. At the end of the corridor, the oases gave way to plains that spread to the edge of the Taklimakan. Early travelers straggling out of the wretched desert breathed a sigh of relief when they reached this point. They knew that, as barren as the area was, the plains led to the greener pastures of the Hexi Corridor.

Noted archaeologist Aurel Stein was one of the last Westerners to explore these tracts before Xinjiang was closed to foreign expeditions in 1930. In 1906-7, in one of six journeys through central Asia, Stein approached the Hexi Corridor from the west and found a mass of brickwork 25 feet high. Realizing that he had found a watchtower of the Great Wall, he followed the remains toward Dunhuang. At the base of one of the towers, he found an inscription in wood confirming that the tower was part of the original, or Han, Wall. Stein described how the towers were constructed of reed bundles fixed with clay and gravel.

Near Dunhuang he visited the temples honeycombed into a hillside that were known as the "Caves of the Thousand Buddhas." Chambers of varying sizes sat one atop the other, inside a 115-foot-high cliff opposite a stream. The caves had been carved throughout the period from the end of the fourth century to the fourteenth century. One of Stein's most famous acquisitions was the selection of religious scrolls and secular documents that had recently been uncovered by a monk at Dunhuang. Nearly 500 man-made caverns testify to the religious dedication of the Buddhists. Buddhism was brought into China via the Silk Road and spread very rapidly.

We crossed Stein's path at the city of Jiayuguan, where our rail passage through the Hexi Corridor ended. Jiayuguan marks the western terminus of the Great Wall, built during the Ming Dynasty (1368-1644). The layer of pebbles and cobbles lying at the base of the huge fortress wall hinted at the origin of the surrounding topography.

The Jiayuguan plain, Dr. Zhao believes, was not fashioned by wind erosion; it had originated as deposits of pebbles brought in by floodwaters from higher ground thousands of years ago. The fortress of Jiayuguan figures prominently in

JIN BOHONG

the folklore of the Silk Road. On the eastern side of this majestic structure, traders and other travelers were protected by the armed forces of Imperial China. Beyond the fortress walls to the west, travelers were left unaided to face dangers from hostile tribes and to cope with demons believed to inhabit the Taklimakan. Legend says that travelers at the fort threw a small pebble against the western gate wall. If the pebble bounced with a ringing sound, the journey began. If the pebble fell with a thud, it signaled a bad omen and travel was postponed to another day. At a second gate, known as "The Weeping Gate," wayfarers shed tears for family members that they had left behind or for friends they might never see again.

We passed through the west gate and entered the storied reaches of the Xinjiang, a frontier of mountains, deserts, and oases. This region constitutes one-sixth of China's total landmass, the homeland of seven ethnic groups of the Islamic faith. The Uygurs, numbering about six million, make up the largest population in this area. They till the flatlands, planting cotton and various vegetables and fruits.

Occupying the foothills of the Altay Mountains are the Kazaks. About a million strong, they graze horses, goats, sheep, and cattle. "Crops produced by these people were not enough for export to more densely populated parts of China," said Liang Kuangyi, a research *(Continued on page 240)*

Termed a "howling wilderness," the Taklimakan appears calm here as two Uygurs from Kashi collect willow and tamarisk for firewood. The forbidding sand sea supports life only on its margins. The scrubby plants survive by growing extensive root systems that draw on meager groundwater. Some human dwellers on the fringe of the desert siphon water from mountain-base aquifers through underground channels called karez.

Wooden bones of a Tang Dynasty town of the seventh to tenth centuries share a stretch of the Taklimakan with a camel train of archaeologists. Shifting dunes suffocated many communities along the southern route of the Silk Road. Fa Xian, a famous Chinese monk who traveled the treacherous route in A.D. 400, noted: "There are evil spirits and hot winds that kill every man who encounters them. . . . As far as the eye can see, no road is visible in the desert, and only the skeletons of those who have perished there serve to mark the way."

JIN BOHONG

233

*P*ut to good use, cobblestones stud the walls of a reservoir under construction (right)—part of a hydroelectric power plant at Yutian in the Taklimakan. The Keriya River from the Kunlun Mountains will supply the water. The Chinese government has encouraged the gradual development of industry and agriculture in this westernmost corner of the country. Known as the Xinjiang Uygur Autonomous Region, the area encompasses one-sixth of China's landmass. Until 1949 the major metallurgical venture here consisted of blacksmithing. Today factories manufacture tractors, such as the red one on the reservoir floor. Below: Outside the nearby oasis town of Hotan, members of a commune screen gravel, a building material easily found. Rocky plains make up 44 percent of China's desert lands. These workers use sifted pebbles and rocks to surface a portion of a highway that loops around the Taklimakan.

JIN BOHONG (BOTH)

234

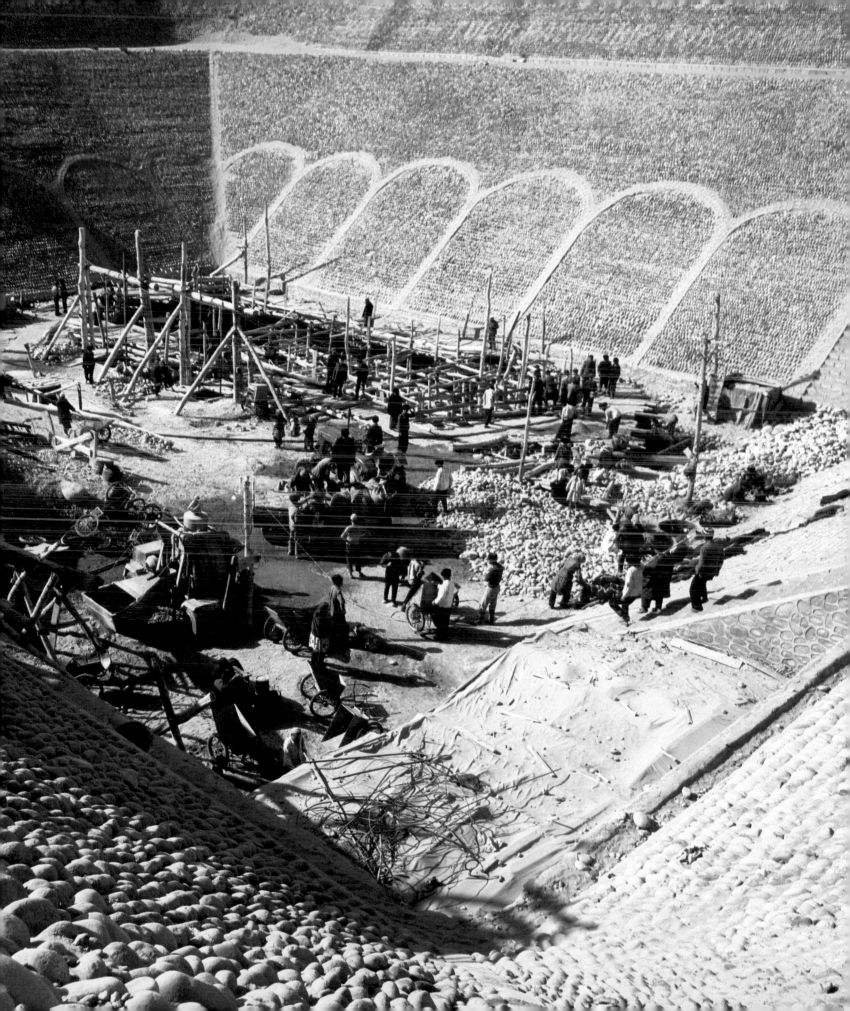

Great Wall of China runs across a gravel plain to Jiayuguan, a 14th-century fortress at the western end of the line built to bar invaders. Opposite: Towers guard the route where caravans once carried silk westward and gold, silver, spices, and precious stones eastward.

FOLLOWING PAGES: *Shocks of hay, bundled like winter soldiers, stand in formation in fields reclaimed by irrigation outside the city of Lanzhou.*

NATIONAL GEOGRAPHIC PHOTOGRAPHER BRUCE DALE (BOTH AND FOLLOWING PAGES).

geologist with the Institute of Geography. "That is why the government established the 'farms.'"

He was referring to the communal outposts where Chinese live and work to reclaim land from the desert. Most of the workers are Han, who make up 94 percent of China's population. The majority of the men and women we met on the desert farms were in their early twenties. Many come from overpopulated cities of eastern China. They live in large single-story buildings that resemble army barracks. They eat together in huge, sparsely furnished dining rooms. They attend political meetings every week and play basketball and table tennis to relax. Life on these farms differs little from the daily regimen of military bases. In fact, one motive for creating the agricultural outposts could have been to establish some protection for China's frontier along the Soviet border. Farm 150, for example, lies in the Gurbantünggüt Desert only 175 miles from the Chinese-Soviet border.

To visit the farm, we drove northwest from the city of Ürümqi. Unpaved, dusty roads lined with poplar trees crisscrossed the agricultural outpost. Workers driving unpainted tractor trucks and bulldozers tilled the fields in orderly procession. One of the farmhands, a woman from Shanghai, had been on the farm for five years.

"Would you like to go back to Shanghai anytime soon?" I asked her.

"If the government asks me, I will go, but life here is much better for me," she answered.

The noise of machinery on Farm 150 contrasted sharply with the serene life in the Uygur-settled Turpan oasis, ten hours to the southeast by car. Out of Ürümqi we followed a wild unpaved track. It led us across bare mountains that surround the 150-mile-wide Turpan Depression.

We descended into the depression, its gently sloping rim a gobi plain, often shrouded by a haze of dust. Because the wind is trapped in the bowl-shaped terrain, dust in the air has no place to go. Consequently, the depression ranks as one of the dustiest and hottest places in the world. Temperatures that exceed 100°F bake the basin, which plummets to 505 feet below sea level, the lowest point in China.

At the center of the Turpan Depression an oasis of melon fields and grape arbors has supported communities since ancient times. Jiaohe, now a ghost city atop a hill, contains Buddhist shrines. The city prospered as a Silk Road outpost and "was eventually conquered by the Uygurs," a local guide told us. These Uygurs coming out of Mongolia ruled from their capital, Gaochang, near Turpan, between the ninth and thirteenth centuries. By the 14th century, the area was converted to Islam.

I explored beyond the edge of the depression's vegetation and discovered a surface where wind had eroded elongated blocks of limestone. The blocks instantly reminded me of the wind-carved rocks found by Swedish explorer Sven Anders Hedin in the desert of Lop Nur, about 150 miles south of Turpan. The Chinese call the rock formations "white dragon hillocks."

Starting in 1890, Hedin—a rugged, self-confident geographer—roamed the virtually unknown lands of the Asian interior. Assisted by Mongols and Uygurs, he first encountered wind-scathed blocks of clay rock 45 miles west of

Revealed as the "great ear of China" by Landsat imagery, dry lake Lop Nur (opposite) marks the eastern end of the Konqi River. Evaporation creates great swirls of white salt and dark sediment, residues that clearly record fluctuations in the level of the lake. Chinese scientists in recent years have used the area of Lop Nur as a testing ground for nuclear weapons.

GEOPIC IMAGES/EARTH SATELLITE CORPORATION

Lop Nur. He wrote in 1903 that his party had come across "a perfect labyrinth of clay 'terraces,' with sharp-cut edges, which the natives called *yardang*; and as this is a very graphic descriptive word, I shall . . . use it when speaking of these scarped formations." Thus the term 'yardang'—from the Turkic word *yar*, "steep bank or cliff"—was coined to describe sharp-crested ridges of soft sediment or solid rock carved by wind erosion.

Hedin correctly recognized that the consistent pattern in the rows of yardangs and the parallel gullies between them in the Lop Nur area indicated that they were formed by the prevailing wind, "which uses the drift-sand as a file against the easily sculptured clay."

"It took us four field seasons plus two more years in the lab to figure out all the dune forms in the Taklimakan," Professor Zhu had said to me earlier. He pointed out that the Taklimakan, which lies in the middle of the Tarim Basin, contains some of the most complex dunes of any sand sea. "The complexity is due to winds that come from two opposing directions—the northeast and the northwest—at the same time," he said. "The two winds meet near the middle of the southern part of the Tarim Basin, and it is here where the dunes really become complex."

The enormous size of the dunes in the Taklimakan has always presented a staggering challenge to wayfarers. The mountains of sand rise as high as 600 feet. For mile after mile, the only visible landmarks are the wavy profiles of

NATIONAL GEOGRAPHIC PHOTOGRAPHER BRUCE DALE (BOTH)

dunes on the shimmering horizon. Many travelers who dared to venture across these shifting dunes lost their way, and some never returned.

"When a man is riding by night," wrote Marco Polo, "and something happens to make him loiter and lose touch with his companions . . . then he hears spirits talking in such a way that they seem to be his companions. . . . Sometimes, indeed, they even hail him by name. . . . make him stray from the path, so that he never finds it again. . . . and often you fancy you are listening to the strains of many instruments, especially drums, and the clash of arms."

I was once mesmerized by the strange singing of a dune in the Sinai desert. "Have you heard such sounds here in China?" I asked Dr. Zhao.

"Yes. It was at the sand mound called Mingsha, which means 'singing sand.' I experienced the sensational sounds when gliding down the dune's slope. The sound was something like the bellowing of many cattle," he said.

At the end of my visit in western China, I waited for a flight at the airport in Ürümqi and pondered the puzzle of the singing dunes. Most experts agree that the eerie sounds begin when layers of sand slide down the side of a dune. But not all sand slides produce such sounds. Could it be that the bouncing of sand grains, under certain atmospheric conditions, generates sounds that shriek, howl, or roar like thunderbolts from clouds? The answer is cloaked in mystery, one of the many desert enigmas yet to be unraveled.

Feathery willow and tamarisk bushes (opposite) cling to dunes near the Yellow River—Huang He—northeast of Lanzhou, a fast-growing industrial city. The tall poplars at river's edge shade buildings of China's Institute of Desert Research. Workers from the facility checkerboard a Tengger Desert dune with straw jammed into the sand in three-foot squares (right). The fishnet pattern stops the drift of the dune by breaking the force of the wind and by confining the movement of sand within the squares. Such efforts have enabled the Chinese to prevent dunes from blowing across a trans-desert railway that links the nation's arid northwestern regions with its eastern heartlands.

JIN BOHONG (ALL)

*O*n a shopping trip (opposite), a Uygur patriarch clutches a
white sack of fruit and vegetables to sell in the free market at
Hotan. In the background stands a state-operated department
store that stocks everything from clothing to toys. For centuries the
Uygurs, who speak a Turkic language, have followed the Muslim
religion. Today some six million Uygurs inhabit Xinjiang, slightly
outnumbering China's major ethnic group, the Han, that live
mainly in the eastern provinces. Uygurs at an outdoor restaurant
in Hotan's marketplace (above) eat a thick stew of lamb, carrots,
and rice. Some of the diners forsake modern utensils and follow
the custom of lifting food to their mouths with the right hand. A
fluffy swatch of untrimmed hide from a mian yang—mountain
sheep—makes a woolly hat that insulates the head of a boy
bundled against the late afternoon chill (left).

244

Asian cowboys, Mongols tend horses on semiarid steppeland fringing the Gobi in Mongolia, an independent republic closely tied to the Soviet Union. The short, stocky legs of the horses reveal animals bred for stamina rather than for speed (right). Below: Galloping after a white colt, a rider uses both hands to grip a long pole with a noose at the end, the Mongolian version of the lasso. Opposite, below: Strong tobacco smoke from a long pipe flavors discussion during a rest break. Although a large number of herdsmen and their families in Mongolia and in China belong to state-controlled communes and live in permanent dwellings, they retain many of their nomadic ways. Few have given up their gers, or yurts, traditional round felt tents kept today for summer homes. In the 13th century under Genghis Khan and his successors, hordes of rugged horsemen extended the Mongol Empire from the east coast of Asia to the Black Sea in the west. Descendants of those conquering armies still occupy ancestral homelands in central Asia's arid lands.

GEORGE HOLTON/OCELOT (ABOVE AND BELOW)

ARA GÜLER—ISTANBUL

247

Heart of a Fiery Frontier

The Outback of Australia

By Thomas O'Neill

Centerpiece of the outback, Ayers Rock glows with sunlight like a live ember. Scarred by climate and time, the giant outcrop abounds in caves, basins, and other features— many considered sacred by Aboriginals, the first people of Australia. Each year the monolith draws thousands of visitors to the dry interior.

ETHAN HOFFMAN

248

Desert rules much of Australia (opposite). Arid and semiarid expanses take up about two-thirds of its landmass. Despite the enormous extent of these areas, Australia lacks the extreme conditions of other continents. Its driest spot— Lake Eyre—averages about four inches of rainfall a year. Moist oceanic air, unhindered by high mountains, penetrates the dry interior and brings sporadic spells of rain. The region wears a surprising visage of vegetation—trees, shrubs, and grasses.

Hyperarid
Arid
Semiarid

It is true, the silence of the desert can make one believe that the beating of the heart is clamorous. And, yes, the air is clear enough that the rising of the moon can startle a camper from sleep. The fabled heat—desiccating, oppressive—is all the imagination said it would be. After traveling one summer in the deserts of Australia, I came to accept as normal the stillness, the raging sun, the crystalline night air, and the bush flies covering my skin and clothes.

What never did cease to amaze me were less dramatic occurrences: a lizard's sudden dart across torrid rock, the twitter of finches from trees around a water hole, the wink of color from a flower on a 110°F day. That life could hang on in a land seemingly so hostile to it was what finally established my wonder.

Arid and semiarid zones cover about two-thirds of Australia, a continent nearly as large as the contiguous United States. Gibson, Great Sandy, Sturt Stony, Great Victoria, Tanami, Simpson: These harsh deserts form part of the country's broad interior. Here the sand often reflects a garish, reddish orange color. The heavily oxidized landscape wears a raw look, as if the top layer of skin had been torn off.

Geographer Jack Mabbutt of the University of New South Wales in Sydney likens the sand deserts of the Australian arid zone to the Kalahari Desert in Africa. "The region is flat because it has been tectonically stable over a long period, though it does have islands of prominent relief and very extensive areas of sand dunes and ridges," he told me.

"There is none of the extreme aridity you'd find in the Sahara," Dr. Mabbutt said. "Even in the heart of it, in the region around Lake Eyre, you're still in areas getting an average of four or five inches of rainfall a year. Partly because of the climate and partly because of the relative lack of human impact, the contrast with the deserts of the Old World is phenomenal. You take Saharanists into the Australian deserts in a reasonable season, and they look around and say, 'Where is the desert?'"

The term "desert" in Australia can seem a misnomer because of the relative abundance of trees and shrubs. Drought-resistant acacias and eucalyptuses add their dusty olive-green color to the brick-red hue of the earth. Even in the most parched region one can find something growing, usually the ubiquitous grasses, *Triodia* and *Plectrachne*, colloquially called spinifex.

Origins of the Australian desert go back an estimated 40 to 50 million years. As the continent was breaking off from Antarctica and moving north into lower latitudes, the buildup of the polar ice cap began cooling the oceans. This set off dramatic climatic changes. As Australia moved north, drier high-pressure zones moved in from the south, gradually increasing aridity. Over time, the level of the oceans dropped, and strong winds blew across the continent, evaporating large inland lakes and piling up sand dunes. Today, too far south to capture rain from the summer monsoons, too far north to receive rainfall from the westerlies in winter, and without high mountains to influence climate substantially, the interior of Australia remains locked in aridity.

Living with a dusty thirst continues to be one of the greatest challenges in Australia's deserts. The slightest rainfall incites celebration. A rainstorm hit when I was visiting Alice Springs, a large outback town with a population of about 18,000. Australia's outback includes vast expanses where relatively few people live. After the overnight downpour a few intersections were flooded, and

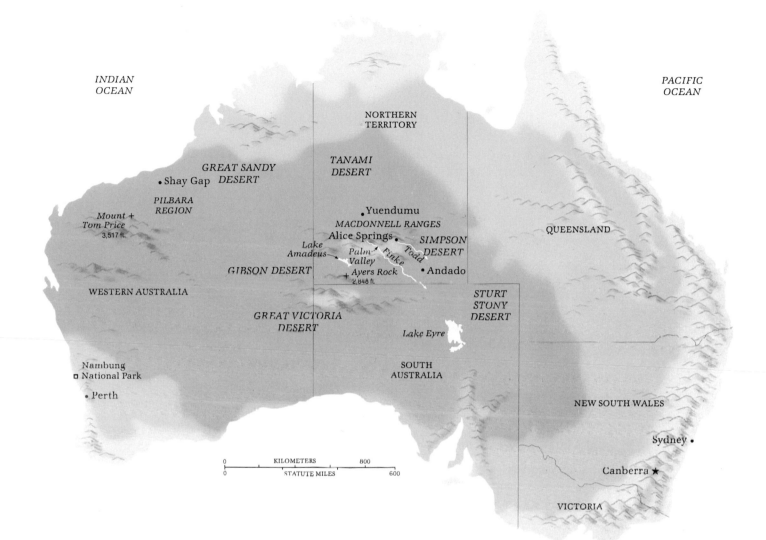

INDIAN
OCEAN

PACIFIC
OCEAN

NORTHERN
TERRITORY

GREAT SANDY
DESERT
• Shay Gap

TANAMI
DESERT

QUEENSLAND

PILBARA
REGION

Mount +
Tom Price
3,517 ft.

• Yuendumu

MACDONNELL RANGES
Alice Springs •
Lake
Amadeus
Palm
Valley
GIBSON DESERT
+ Ayers Rock
2,848 ft.

SIMPSON
DESERT

• Andado

WESTERN AUSTRALIA

GREAT VICTORIA
DESERT

STURT
STONY
DESERT

Lake Eyre

Nambung
National Park

SOUTH
AUSTRALIA

• Perth

NEW SOUTH WALES

Sydney •

KILOMETERS   800
0
STATUTE MILES
0   600

Canberra ★

VICTORIA

TASMANIA

desert roads had dissolved into mud. People were talking: "The Todd River is running. First time in months." What I saw was not a torrent, but a sluggish rivulet coursing down the riverbed. Children splashed in the puddles; the event made front-page news. Such is the thrill of rain in the desert. Two days later the Todd was dry again.

To endure the parched environment of the Australian arid zone, plants and animals have developed fascinating mechanisms for survival. The seeds of Sturt's desert pea can lie inactive in the soil for many years in wait for a substantial rain. When it comes, the seeds germinate into plants that send forth glossy red-and-black petals. As for animals, there are frogs that bloat their bodies with water and dig themselves cooler hideaways underground. The fat-tailed dunnart, one of Australia's small marsupials, stores food in its tail.

Humans have developed adaptive devices as well, ones fashioned from wits and fortitude rather than from genetic finesse. Masters at desert survival are the Aboriginals, the first people of Australia. Of the continent's present population of about 15 million, approximately 180,000 are Aboriginals. These brown-skinned hunters and gatherers first inhabited Australia at least 30,000

DEREK ROFF

ROBIN SMITH

Mythic traveler, the emu appears in an Aboriginal cave painting (above) at a site in the central desert. Cave paintings such as this one can depict mythological stories. The Aboriginals make use of ochers, charcoal, and ash for drawing materials. Fast and flightless, the emu (left) remains a prize food for Aboriginals.

years ago. Skilled at tracking—today the Aboriginals have learned to read tire tracks—the men went after such prey as kangaroos, emus, bustards, and lizards. Women collected fruits and other plant foods.

"A mobile people, the Aboriginals essentially chased rain," explains archaeologist Richard Gould of Brown University. "With rain showers visible up to 50 miles away in the desert, Aboriginals traveling in groups of 20 to 30 could relate the location of the rain to their precise knowledge of where water catchments and staple-food plants existed."

To minimize risk, the Aboriginals made few random trips. Their unerring movement has been observed by American anthropologist Dr. Fred Myers. He lived with the Pintupi people in the Gibson Desert as part of his work under a grant from the Australian Institute of Aboriginal Studies in Canberra.

"They know nearly every spot where a desert yam would be growing," Dr. Myers explained to me, "or where bush currants were, so they could schedule their movements to reach areas when the plants were ready to be exploited. They have never just wandered in the desert."

There is a saying in the outback that goes: "When things are good, they're bloody good; when things are bad, they're awful." This maxim can be applied to the desert Aboriginals. Though hard-pressed during droughts, in moderate years the Aboriginals can give lie to the notion that they barely scrape by. Professor Gould has calculated that food gathering often consumes no more than a maximum of six to seven hours a day, leaving ample time for other favored activities such as chatting, toolmaking, and rituals.

Eager to come face-to-face with these resilient people, I summoned the aid of Richard Kimber, a high-school history teacher from Alice Springs. Out of his own curiosity, Dick had been visiting the Warlpiri and Pintupi people for ten years. One November morning, at a distance of 175 miles northwestward from Alice Springs, Dick and I wheeled our pickup into Yuendumu, dusty home to about one thousand Aboriginals south of the Tanami Desert in central Australia. The federal government, which funds the settlement, had erected rows of concrete-block houses. Many were unused; some of the people preferring to live in humpies—traditional-style shelters that rise like termite mounds on the outskirts of the settlement. The humpies were mainly lean-tos constructed with a hodgepodge of materials, mostly corrugated metal, tree boughs, and tarpaulins. One builder had turned a car hood into a wall for his home.

As we drove through camp, we came to an area where several men indicated that they wished to accompany us into the bush. Each announced to the woman at his shelter that he was leaving, picked up his bedroll (swag) and tea bucket (billycan), and climbed into the pickup bed. The men delighted in returning to the open desert, if only for a few days.

Few Aboriginals still live in the bush, free of contact with towns or settlements. Starting about the 1880s the Aboriginals of central Australia began to drift into the "whitefella's world"—cattle stations, mining camps, and settlements—in search of supplies during droughts. By the 1960s the desert was virtually emptied of its traditional desert dwellers; many of them had moved into settlements by this time. Once exposed to the white man's more easily available supplies of flour, steel axes, sugar, rifles, *(Continued on page 256)*

*I*nto the cooking pit goes one of six kangaroos bagged by a group of Pintupi Aboriginals in the Gibson Desert. Ritual leader Nosepeg Tjupurula stands ready with a stick to spread the coals. Aboriginals venture into the open desert to chase down 'roos, a favorite food, and to visit sacred sites. These people believe that the landscape contains the essence of mythological beings who created life during a period known as the Dreaming. Although most of the country's Aboriginals now live in cities or in government-funded settlements, the establishment of outstations, small family outposts in the desert, may help Aboriginals stay close to ancestral lands.

ETHAN HOFFMAN (BELOW AND FAR RIGHT)

ERIC R. PIANKA

drinking water, and medicine, the Aboriginals found it difficult to return to their traditional life.

"Settlements were like big water holes to the Aboriginals, but they didn't foresee the consequences," Dr. Myers told me. "The people saw their autonomy decline. Their emphasis on hunting and gathering ways diminished as they became dependent on the material goods on trading-post shelves."

Some positive aspects have emerged, however, such as the intensification of religious and social life. Also, groups in the last ten years have begun to move away from the settlements to establish outstations. Though still supplied from the settlement, an outstation allows the inhabitants to come in closer contact with the totemic country, landscape invested with deep religious meaning.

"Bring back *marlu!*" a man shouted to our pickup crew as we headed out of Yuendumu. He wanted kangaroo, still one of the favorite meats of the Aboriginals. Frank Tjakamara and Mick Tjampitjinpa were more than glad to oblige. The youngest of the group, both in their 30s, they cradled .22-caliber rifles in their arms. All but vanished is the image of Aboriginals who walk around the desert naked, hefting spears and boomerangs. Most of them now wear Western clothes. Sometimes the effect seems out of character, as in the case of Frank, a bulky fellow whose outfit consisted of blue shorts, red socks, brown leather shoes, and a yellow T-shirt with a picture of a motorcycle. Little changed, however, is the Aboriginals' interest in hunting. In the scrub, two hours out of Yuendumu, Frank and Mick went into action. They killed a kangaroo and a bustard, a large bird.

"This is my country," Jack Tjampitjinpa said, shyly waving his hand toward the land outside the window of the pickup. Jack, an elderly Aboriginal with a white beard, and another Warlpiri elder, Jim Tjupurula, began talking excitedly in their language. They pointed long fingers into the distance. I squinted my eyes against the blazing sun and took in a panorama of burnt earth, shrubby trees, and tower-shaped termite mounds. The country looked little different from what we had seen for the past three hours. But the land for Jack abounded in sacred sites. This was totemic country, the traditional domain of Jack's family, the place that empowers him and his relatives with its spirit.

D eeply religious, the Aboriginals hold that great beings of creation live eternally in beliefs and rituals called the Dreaming. "Snake Dreaming," one of the riders called out as we bounced across a dry creek, the winding path taken by a Dreaming snake. We moved on to a campsite of the Dreaming kangaroo.

"That's where the marlu slept," whispered Dinny Tjapaltjari, his thick sand-colored hair shaking in the light wind. He was pointing to a depression in the rock. "That's where he traveled." He was looking toward a white streak in the rock where, he said, the kangaroo had dragged its tail.

The Aboriginals owe much of their uncommon desert savvy to their concept of the Dreaming—the extraordinary period of creation when mythic creatures with interchangeable human and animal features undertook heroic journeys across the earth, shaping the landscape, giving life to plants and animals, introducing human life and culture. In a sense, the Dreaming never ended. Wherever the mythic travelers stopped, they left the essence of their spirits. If an Aboriginal is conceived or born in the country where, say, the emu passed in the Dreaming, the child supposedly absorbs the living spirit of the place and is said to have become part of the emu's Dreaming.

This mythology acts as a code for reality. The stories, often intricate and full of imagery, set down by example the rituals and beliefs the Aboriginals observe in their society. The tales especially instruct the people to care for their country, since the land, the plants, the animals, and the humans all share the same spirits.

The Dreaming tracks of some totemic beings, such as the kangaroo and the snake, extend for several hundred miles. These paths in effect create a desert network in which people from different groups become kinsmen, since they belong to the same Dreaming. This alliance can prove beneficial during droughts by allowing an affected group to move without tension into another's territory where dependable water might be available. The Dreaming tracks also help account for the uncanny ability of Aboriginals to find their way across a terrain essentially trackless to the untrained eye. As part of the initiation process, young Aboriginals must memorize the Dreaming tales. Knowledge of the specific tracks equips the initiate with an indelible mental map. He can chart a path without relying solely on the sun or on any compass point. He

Strategic digging at a lizard burrow (opposite) yields a plump sand goanna for a mother and her two daughters, fair-haired like some Aboriginal children. The sharp-clawed reptile—a type of monitor lizard—grows several feet in length and serves as a source of meat for the desert people. A witchetty grub, or insect larva, makes a desert delicacy for the Aboriginals. A girl (above) searches for an insect larva in a desert poplar. A favorite snack, the moth larva (below) tastes somewhat like creamy butter when eaten raw. The desert Aboriginals also turn for food to various plants growing in the outback. They long ago mastered the art of survival in the harsh lands.

© RICK SMOLAN/CONTACT STOCK IMAGES

depends also on the various landmarks that might figure in a tale's narrative.

The Dreaming tales opened my eyes. I looked at the desert anew. A pile of boulders was the camping site of a lizard man. A rock hole was the home of a rainbow serpent. The large barren expanse of Lake Eyre was the spot where a Dreaming man had flung down a kangaroo skin.

Colorful stories spring from Ayers Rock, a well-known site of Aboriginal faith. The famous sandstone monolith measures 5½ miles around its base and rises 1,143 feet above its surrounding plain. Many features of the imposing outcrop relate to mythology.

One of the most rousing tales is the attack on the peaceful carpet snakes, *Kunia*, by the poisonous snakes, *Liru*. The topography on the rock's southern face tells the story: Advancing are the Liru (desert oaks standing off from the rock). Liru are hurling spears (pits on the rock wall). Shouting sounds come from the invaders' mouths (caves in the rock). A Kunia man and a Liru man square off. The carpet snake twice slashes the leg of his enemy; the blood flows from the two fissures on the rock's wall. But the Liru man eventually prevails. The Kunia man bleeds to death (his spilled blood is the water standing in three rock holes).

The carpet snake's mother, hearing of her son's death, becomes violently angry and with a digging stick cuts off the Liru man's nose (a large slab of rock that has split off from the side of Ayers Rock. Dark patches of lichens on the rock face are blood pouring from the dying man). The poisonous snakes finally overwhelm the Kunia, and on the summit of Ayers Rock appear the bodies of the vanquished (cylindrical boulders that glow scarlet in the setting sun).

A dying sun beating against our pickup hastened our awareness of hunger and thirst. I stopped the pickup. While a few of the men started a fire to heat a charred billycan, Dinny Tjapaltjari picked up an ax, walked over to a tree on the bank of a dry creek bed, and started to hack at it. Soon he pulled from the tree a large, white, fleshy larva—that Aboriginal delicacy known as a witchetty grub. Dinny repeated the process a few times and then cheerfully shared the grubs. Each one measured about an inch long. They were quickly consumed raw. Dinny said they tasted like a helping of creamy eggs. With no more exertion than if they had carved their names on a trunk, the men had secured for themselves a snack and were ready to sit down in the dirt to late afternoon tea.

That night the Aboriginals prepared the kangaroo that Frank and Mick had shot. They placed it in a pit and covered it with embers. Hours later the men lifted the cooked kangaroo from the ember pit, cut it up in a prescribed manner, and handed it out. They allocated pieces according to a strict code for sharing food. Dick and I were presented the tail. These Aboriginals believed that we would prefer this part. The meat was slightly raw and gamy, but nutritious. After the meal I fell asleep next to a flickering campfire. Never had I felt more secure in the wilderness than I did with this small group of desert people.

Being alone without food or drink is a desert traveler's greatest danger. To overcome such privation, a human can stomach almost any solution. A case in point is Ernest Giles, a 19th century English explorer who traversed Australia's fearsome western deserts. During a trip in 1874, separated from his companions, his food and water used up several days before, Giles was doubtful whether he could go on. *(Continued on page 268)*

Nearly devoid of life, the Sturt Stony Desert (opposite), with its torrid rock-strewn surface, bears the name of Charles Sturt, an explorer who came upon this rugged land in the 1840s during the last of three expeditions. The Sturt Stony Desert ranks as one of Australia's most barren landscapes. This wasteland formed over many years as wind and water disintegrated the rocky underlying crust.

FOLLOWING PAGES: *Fiery dunes flow across the Simpson Desert in the Northern Territory. Such parallel dunes often dominate Australia's sand deserts.*

ROBIN SMITH (OPPOSITE);
ETHAN HOFFMAN (FOLLOWING PAGES)

*M*ottled in complexion
when viewed from a satellite, the
*Great Sandy Desert in Western
Australia exhibits a mix of
sand, rock, and vegetation.
Parallel striations of sand ridges
typical of Australia's desert
dune fields give the image a
lacework look. The dense areas
across the lower right represent
low hills, bare rock, and sand
dunes. To the northwest, a salt
flat adds a daub of white to
this parched zone.*

GEOPIC IMAGES/EARTH SATELLITE CORPORATION

Called Katatjurta, or "many heads," by the Aboriginals, the sunlit Olgas stand as a great island of stone in the

GEORG GERSTER

majestic remoteness of the Northern Territory near Ayers Rock.

*F*ury of a dust storm descends on Alice Springs, an outback town in central Australia. A dust cloud engulfed the community after years of extreme dryness had left insufficient vegetation to hold the soil in the high wind. To anchor topsoil, scientists have begun a project of planting grasses around Alice Springs. Undaunted by the desert, the town musters such amusements as the annual Henley-on-Todd regatta (below). Crews race a variety of leg-driven craft down the dry bed of the Todd River.

JEFF CARTER (ABOVE); ROBIN SMITH (RIGHT)

Then, "I heard a faint squeak, and looking about I saw, and immediately caught, a small dying wallaby, whose marsupial mother had evidently thrown it from her pouch. . . . The instant I saw it, like an eagle I pounced upon it and ate it, living, raw, dying—fur, skin, bones, skull, and all. The delicious taste of that creature I shall never forget."

Another explorer, John McDouall Stuart, accomplished one of the first south-north traverses of the continent in the early 1860s. He had been commissioned specifically to scout for suitable pastoral land. Stuart's expedition happened to coincide with a moderately wet time, and his reports were generally favorable. His reports and the completion of the Overland Telegraph Line in 1872 encouraged settlers to push into the arid interior.

Sheep and cattlemen came to these areas in the mid-to-late 1800s. They saw a pasture amid the spinifex, and they wished to put as many domestic herds on it as possible. They carved much of the outback into huge ranches, called stations. The early pastoralists, however, soon learned that the essence of Australia's desert climate is an alternation between good seasons and drought. A terrible dry spell in the 1890s practically wiped them out.

Other difficulties presented themselves to the ranchers: skirmishes with the Aboriginals; the tyranny of long distances; transporting cattle to markets 30 days or more away by trail. Furthermore, the market itself was finicky, a day's difference in price determining success or failure for the year.

It took a self-sacrificing and, most important, a lucky individual to make a go of it in those days. A pioneer's son wrote: "It has been said that those who go out into the great open spaces of Australia have great open spaces in their heads. However that may be, their hearts are full of the right stuff." With gritty perseverance, the toughest ranchers kept their stock alive on the desert pasture of grasses, herbage, and browse. Today about 500,000 head of cattle graze on 80 stations in central Australia. Arid and semiarid ranches account for about 20 percent of the continent's exports of wool and beef.

The graziers remain hardworking individualists. I once arrived five minutes late for an appointment with a station owner and found him pulling out of the yard in a pickup. Since I did not show precisely at eight o'clock, he informed me tersely, he had decided to leave. He said that chores on his 600,000-acre spread took precedence over polite conversation with a stranger. I looked at his weathered black fedora on the seat next to him. The man's eyes were pale blue and hard, his forearms thick and dustbrown. What could I say?

When I finally did converse with the station owner, he presented an understated appraisal of the early cattlemen's existence, observing that they took life as it came. He also made clear his own enduring toughness. Sitting inside his air-conditioned, thick-carpeted front room, he explained that the pioneers were much hardier than people today, but that he still considered himself part of that ancestral breed. He stated that he never expected a drink in the desert. Even if he got dry in the mouth, he said, he just kept at his work without complaint. He wouldn't say the same for his sons. He had long known that the customary pastoral life in the outback follows a boom-and-bust cycle. In bust times, when extreme aridity seems to crack the sky, the cattlemen cling to optimism. "It will come good," is their slogan for the land.

ETHAN HOFFMAN

"When you see this country in a good year," said Jock Nelson, a former cattleman and later mayor of Alice Springs, "it's like the Garden of Eden. It's some of the sweetest cattle country in Australia."

The country indeed can be sweet. The natural grasses are nourishing, and there are relatively few serious diseases or biting insects to worry the stock. "Cattle raising can be easy here. It's like harvesting a crop," one old-timer told me. In spinifex sand-plain country, the ratio of cattle to each square mile is less than one; on the good alluvial land in the arid zone, the number reaches 20 per square mile. In some grazing areas outside the desert, by contrast, the ratio leaps to more than a hundred beasts every square mile.

Larger than the state of Connecticut, Andado Station sprawls 6,362 square miles across the fringe of the Simpson Desert in central Australia, where red sand dunes run in parallel lines for miles and miles. The spread is one of the largest privately managed stations in the area. The main fare of conversation in November 1980 was the dry weather. "The dust storms are coming back," observed Kevin Clark, who with his brother Philip runs the station. "There have been five in the last few months." (Continued on page 272)

"This infernal lake ... a perfect bog," explorer Ernest Giles called Lake Amadeus (above) in 1872. Where rivers of central Australia may have once drained, the 90-mile-long lake today has a white salt crust containing briny mud flats and salt-rimmed islands of vegetation. Water from recent rains adds a short-lived blue sheen.

GEORG GERSTER

*G*iant furrows etch the Macdonnell Ranges of Australia's Northern Territory (left). Between the harder quartzite ribs of rock lie valleys eroded from softer sandstone and shale. Below: Cabbage palms tap moisture in Palm Valley in the area. Bottom: Dry-climate grasses, commonly called spinifex, need no oasis.

BARRY ALLWRIGHT

ROBIN SMITH

"We'll have to get down to 1,500 to 2,000 head of cattle if the conditions stay bad," said Philip. In good times Andado will carry 13,000 head.

The Clark family had weathered close to a decade of drought through the 1960s. Sand had piled up as high as the roofs of their cars. The long dry spell of those years was followed by tumultuous rains; in two years 30 inches fell. Creeks and rivers flooded. A low-lying area near the house went 20 feet deep in places. The Clarks called it "the lake." Their children swam in it; various birds flocked to it.

Not able to count on such a bonanza in the unreliable seasons of arid Australia, the Clarks were now proceeding as if a drought had come to stay. One of the brothers regularly checks the bores. These wells have helped alleviate the boom-and-bust regimen by giving pastoralists year-round access to deep underground water. But, if a bore engine shuts down unnoticed, and no water is being pumped, 800 cattle could die in a day.

It was bore-inspection day. I joined Philip, a tall, quiet blond with deep lines like sand dunes radiating from his eyes. He took the station's single-engine plane up. In an hour of flying, we passed over wave after wave of sand dunes, flat, hard-baked stretches of stony desert, and over the Finke River, where an outburst of coolibah trees resembled a forest against the desert's gravel. All the bores were working, their windmills pumping priceless water.

Philip swooped low in an unsuccessful look for feral camels sighted a few days earlier. Introduced in the 19th century to aid exploration, dromedaries have thrived in the outback. Philip banked our plane back toward Andado. The seemingly boundless outback tilting away toward an empty horizon made me realize another problem of living on a station: isolation. The nearest neighbor to Andado lives 50 miles away. Yet the station occupants have adapted well. The Clarks' children take lessons from the School of the Air, which broadcasts to Andado over a two-way radio from Alice Springs, about 150 miles away. A mail plane delivers perishables once a week. The news-and-weather report comes by radio. And the Royal Flying Doctor Service tends to the emergency medical needs of the family.

Kerry Clark and her cousin Dulcie, Philip's wife, stay sociable by visiting Alice Springs at least once every three months. "You don't need much of an excuse to go to Alice," says Dulcie, who devotes a great deal of her time to cooking and laundering. "I like to brush the cobwebs away and to go to the club for tea."

Months after my visit, Dick Kimber sent me a postscript to the drought. His letter reported that 5½ inches of rain had fallen on Andado in one week. The bone-dry creek flooded, and the Clarks were forced to sandbag their homes. "Bloody amazing, and yet that's how the desert works," Dick wrote.

In addition to ranchers, Australia attracted a different breed of adventurer: the miner. Gold rushes in the mid and late 1800s led to exploration in the deserts, and to discoveries of silver, lead, zinc, and copper. Uranium, aluminum, nickel, and iron played roles in the post-World War II mineral boom. One of the most active mining areas nowadays is the Pilbara, a region with huge deposits of iron ore southwest of the Great Sandy Desert in the state of Western Australia. Here residents live with blowing dust and high temperatures. To

NATIONAL GEOGRAPHIC PHOTOGRAPHER JAMES L. STANFIELD

meet the challenge of the environment, one company, Goldsworthy Mining Limited, of Perth, has taken an ambitious, novel step. In an area where cyclones can rage and temperatures can soar above 100°F, Goldsworthy Mining built Shay Gap, an experimental town that helps its inhabitants pretend the desert hardly exists at all.

Shay Gap clusters inside a 270-degree arc of ironstone hills, literal relief in a landscape of vast, flat plains. In this natural amphitheater, the houses of Shay Gap huddle tightly and resemble futuristic mobile homes with shiny white polyurethane walls, porthole-like windows, and boxy uniform shapes.

Built in 1972, the town was influenced in its design by the walled cities of the Middle East. Perth architect Lawrence Howroyd chose the bowl of hills to serve as the town's walls, hoping they would provide shade and block hot easterly winds. Houses were placed close together to encourage social contact among the residents. At midday, with a breeze (Continued on page 282)

Tearing open a hill in the Hamersley Range area, miners unearth a wealth of iron ore at Mount Tom Price in Western Australia. The high-grade ore goes to steelmakers in Japan. Vast reserves of iron ore have encouraged mining in Australia's Pilbara region.

GEORG GERSTER (BOTH)

*L*ow rider in the sky rounds up cattle at
Andado Station (left). Australians call a
roundup a muster. The huge ranch sprawls
at the edge of the Simpson Desert for more
than 6,000 square miles, an area larger
than Connecticut. Despite help from an
airborne wrangler, it still takes the
traditional horseman on the ground to
hold the herd, or mob, together. Following
muster, station hands at a portable corral,
or yard, pin down a steer to dehorn it and
ready it for transport to market (above).
Decent cattle country exists in the
outback's center, a region relatively free of
pests and serious disease. Drought poses
inevitable problems, though, forcing
pastoralists to live with boom-and-bust
cycles. They may prosper during rainy
periods and suffer through hard dry spells.

*L*ate afternoon light lingers over Andado Station. Fifty miles from the nearest neighbor, 150 miles from Alice Springs, Andado imposes isolation on its proprietors—the Clarks. Right: On the radio, an important link with the outside world, Dulcie Clark takes a telegram from the Royal Flying Doctor Service, which can supply medical care by airplane. Children at Andado can attend classes at home; they tune in the School of the Air to receive lessons over two-way radio sets. Far right: Philip Clark, wearing a hat, works at a bore, a windmill-powered well that pumps water for cattle on the dry range. Galahs, a kind of cockatoo, queue up for a drink (far right, below).

ETHAN HOFFMAN (BELOW, RIGHT, AND BOTTOM)

© RICK SMOLAN/CONTACT STOCK IMAGES

*S*cars of erosion vanish under patches of green at a land reclamation project in New South Wales (right). Overgrazing stripped the land of topsoil, leaving a hard layer of clay. Constructed ponding banks now retain seeds and water, enabling vegetation to reclaim the surface. Top: At Fowlers Gap Arid Zone Research Station of the University of New South Wales, motorbike and sheep dog team up to muster a flock of merinos, which often share their range with kangaroos. Nuisances for pastoralists include rabbits that pop out of their burrows (above) and devour grasses.

GEORG GERSTER (ALL)

PRECEDING PAGES: *Limestone pinnacles create a cemetery-like expanse at Nambung National Park in Western Australia.*

Blessed with rainfall, billy-buttons burst into bloom around an Eremophila *shrub (opposite). Below: Sturt's desert pea responds to moisture with brilliant flowers. The plant's hard-cased seeds can lie dormant for many years waiting for water. Bottom: On a scorching day, a spinifex hopping-mouse meets the desert challenge by resting in a cool burrow.*

F. COLLET/ARDEA LONDON

M. K. AND I. M. MORCOMBE

JEAN-PAUL FERRERO/ARDEA LONDON
(PRECEDING PAGES)

mollifying a 104°F temperature, I walked through the quiet town of 906 people. Amid the houses I found a school, a small shopping complex, a large swimming pool, a cricket field, tennis courts, shaded walkways, an outdoor movie theater, and a social club. Shay Gap was certainly an oasis, one that looked like an American college campus.

Goldsworthy Mining built Shay Gap with the desire not only to screen out the desert but also to reduce a mining town's traditionally high employee turnover. Many miners are transients in the desert, sharing the pecuniary motives of Joe Atkins. "I'm here to make as much chaff [money] as I can," said Joe. "I'm saving for a good house. I'll stay for 12 months."

To bring stability to the community and to entice its employees to remain longer than a year, Goldsworthy has worked hard to recruit families and to provide them with an acceptable social life. In 1980 close to 50 percent of the adult population at Shay Gap was married. Clive Mills, 26, and his wife, Thelma, 25, had intended to stay for a year and then take the money and run. When I met them in their home, where the rent is subsidized and the electricity and water are free, the Millses were going on year four. Both were enthusiastic about town activities. "I play rugby, soccer, and basketball," said Clive. "On weekends I go fishing in the Indian Ocean about 40 miles away, or I take to the hills in my four-wheel-drive vehicle."

Thelma spoke up. "I find Shay Gap better than where I lived before in Queensland. I didn't see friends as much then. They were too far away."

The company has also endeavored to hire more single women. Unmarried women are now driving trucks, working on blast crews, and serving as assistants to tradesmen. "I was here before the girls came," said township officer Ian Stewart. "Saturday night at the club was like a Wild West scene. You couldn't walk out of the club after 11:30 without getting into a fight. I'll tell you, now there's less fighting, less argument. Altogether, it's now a much more pleasant place in which to live."

And thus, in its own way, Shay Gap continues to court normalcy despite its remote location and harsh climate.

Because man lives on a teetering balance in the desert, the penalty paid for a lapse in mental judgment or physical alertness can be serious. I found this out in a modest way on a blistering November afternoon. Dick Kimber and I were driving a pickup across a sun-baked track in Australia's Tanami Desert. I swerved to miss a goanna, a large speckled lizard that crossed our path. The wheels of our tilting vehicle hit loose sand. We tipped over.

Tangled in the upended cab, Dick and I were shaken but not hurt. We climbed out and tried to right the pickup, but couldn't. We retreated to the shade of a small tree and sat quietly for a long time. Our vulnerability in the immense desert became glaringly apparent. I shuddered and scanned the bleak terrain for any sign of rescue. Nothing.

Hours passed. A movement caught my eye. A shadowy form shimmered in the flat distance. A mirage? It loomed closer, a truck spilling over with Aboriginals. It stopped, and five men jumped down and helped us right our pickup. The Aboriginals would not leave until we demonstrated that our vehicle would run. The engine fired up. We signaled OK and continued humbly on our way.

Secrets of Living in Arid Lands

The following pages reveal some of the ways plants, animals, and humans exist in hot lands with very little water. Plants and animals depend mainly on physiological adaptations for survival; humans rely more on cultural and technological solutions.

Thick adobe walls (below) in the Sahara provide insulation. Tiny, high windows eclipse the blazing sunlight and help keep out dust.

THOMAS J. ABERCROMBIE, NATIONAL GEOGRAPHIC STAFF

TOR EIGELAND

GENEROUS HOSPITALITY: LAW OF THE DESERT

In the desert, where hospitality can mean survival, a Jordanian policeman (left) prepares coffee and tea in a Bedouin tent.

An elaborate welcome for guests remains the law of the desert—even enemies can stay in camp for three days. For the Bedouin, lavish generosity signifies a man's honor.

After an exchange of extended greetings and several cups of coffee and tea comes the sharing of essential news: where to find good grazing and water.

Such traditions lend stability to the nomads' lives as they continually move with their herds and flocks.

TOR EIGELAND

OCEAN ENRICHES A THIRSTY LAND

Turning sardines to dry, an Omani near the city of Salalah puts the heat of the sun to work. Drying will take only a day or two, then most of the fish will go to market as camel fodder or as fertilizer.

Gravel flats and hot, sandy desert cover much of the Sultanate of Oman. The country's thousand-mile coastline, however, fronts deep waters rich in nutrients that support an abundance of fish.

From about 2000 B.C. people along this coast have exploited the ocean. Early Omanis sailed as far as the Orient with cargoes of sharks. Chinese prized these imported fish for their special delicacy, sharkfin soup.

Omani life has continually shifted between the outward call of the sea and the inward tug of oasis agriculture in the nation's dry and isolated interior.

LYNN ABERCROMBIE

COMMUNITY'S WEALTH MEASURED BY WATER

Open-air market in Nazwa, traditional capital of Oman, bustles with farmers selling alfalfa grown in irrigated plots. Ownership of water rights forms the economic and social base of Oman's oasis towns. The rights, sometimes inherited, consist of blocks of time for drawing water from a canal. This carefully controlled system prevents waste. In rainy years, villagers gather in the marketplace and bid for supplies of surplus water.

GEORG GERSTER

HERDERS HEAD FOR GREENER PASTURES

Overgrazing vegetation and trampling the soil with their hooves, cattle contribute to the spread of the Sahara. The relentlessly encroaching desert has forced many herders to leave parts of the Sahel savanna, which lies on the southern edge of the Sahara.

NATIONAL GEOGRAPHIC PHOTOGRAPHER JAMES P. BLAIR

ANCIENT "MOBILE HOME" SHELTERS NOMADS

Packable and portable, the tent remains the traditional shelter of Baluchi nomads (left) of Iran. Although the black cloth absorbs heat, the tent's loose woolen weave permits ventilation. Inside, the temperature stays as much as 30°F cooler than outside. In winter, large, straw mats close off the entrance of the tent and deflect cold wind.

MAN-MADE CANYONS CREATE CITY SHADE

Richly carved mansions cast cool shadows—welcome relief for cows and pedestrians who amble down a stone-paved street in Jaisalmer, a city in the Great Indian Desert.

Desert townspeople often make comfortable avenues of shade by constructing tall buildings on both sides of narrow streets. Clustered tightly, many of the buildings in Jaisalmer share common walls. Such construction decreases the amount of surface exposed to the sun. Dense, thick walls provide additional insulation, and during the day heavy shutters bar the hot sunlight. Often, the houses open onto shaded central courtyards; covered balconies catch breezes.

Built on a camel trail in 1156, the walled city served as the capital of the state of Jaisalmer until India achieved independence from Great Britain in 1947. Now most of the 20,000 inhabitants farm nearby scrubland.

A large part of the Great Indian Desert, also called the Thar, receives only enough rain to support one crop each year. Farmers sow wheat in early winter or millet during the summer monsoon season.

The struggle to scratch a living from the desert, however, has accelerated its spread, especially in the last hundred years. Animals overgraze pastures, and woodcutters clear the land of trees. Much greener 5,000 years ago, the Thar now covers almost half of India's northwest corner.

GEORG GERSTER

NATIONAL GEOGRAPHIC PHOTOGRAPHER GEORGE F. MOBLEY

NATIONAL GEOGRAPHIC PHOTOGRAPHER BRUCE DALE

NATIONAL GEOGRAPHIC PHOTOGRAPHER JAMES L. STANFIELD

CLIFF DWELLINGS
AND HOMES OF EARTH

For thousands of years, Indians in the southwestern United States have used materials at hand to construct a life in harmony with an arid or semiarid environment.

Indians known as the Anasazi—the Ancient Ones—built elaborate stone towns in caves high in canyon walls, such as Cliff Palace at Mesa Verde (left), in present-day Colorado. The semiarid climate permitted dry farming, perhaps atop the mesa, but rain fell erratically. Some archaeologists believe a succession of droughts, culminating in one that lasted from 1276 to 1299, forced the residents to abandon the town.

The Navajo, nomads who had migrated to the area from the Canadian Northwest, chose less permanent dwellings. Their homes, called hogans (left, center), developed from a round tepee-like shelter made of forked sticks leaning together, covered with bark, leaves, and grass. The Indians adapted this structure, designed for a wet climate, to the dry Southwest by covering it with a layer of earth. The thick earthen walls and roof keep indoor temperatures cooler in summer and warmer in winter. Hogans proved such a successful adaptation that many Navajo still live in them today.

FREE SUNSHINE
CUTS FUEL BILLS

Glass panels on the roof of a house in Tucson, Arizona, collect solar energy and transfer it to a circulation system that provides low-cost heat and hot water, and even warms the swimming pool. Solar-heated water also serves as an energy source for air-conditioning the house.

People in this region have used passive heating systems powered by the sun since ancient times. Modern solar technology, however, still requires considerable refinement. Arizona—the sunniest state in the U.S.—stages contests and gives tax incentives to encourage the design of practical solar-energy houses.

GEORG GERSTER

WRAPPED
FOR COMFORT

Bella tribesmen in Upper Volta, once serfs of the Tuareg, wear turbans similar to those of their former masters. The white wrapping reflects sunlight. Sunglasses add a modern touch.

The cotton veil guards the face against stinging sand in the windblown desert. It also traps exhaled breath, creating a humid air pocket around the face that keeps the nose and mouth from drying out.

GEORG GERSTER

AFRICAN BUSHMEN
TRAP ELUSIVE FOOD

Looping a cord around a trimmed sapling, a Bushman readies a noose to snare such wild game as small antelopes. These people have survived in the Kalahari Desert of Africa for more than 20,000 years. Hunters and gatherers, they comb the sandveld on foot for food. They travel light, wearing little clothing. During the heat of midday they rest in shallow, covered pits dug into the ground. The Bushmen's darkly pigmented skin offers some protection from the ultraviolet radiation of the desert sun.

TOR EIGELAND

FLOWING ROBES
AIR-COOL BODIES

Functional desert dress, a white robe covers an Omani almost completely (left), protecting him from the hot, burning rays of the sun.

Throughout the Middle East, loose, tentlike clothing—the *dishdasha* in Oman, the *thawb* in Saudi Arabia, and the *galabia* in Egypt—permits air to circulate inside the flowing robe, which creates a cushion of air around the body. Evaporation of moisture from the skin produces a cooling effect.

Like this tribesman, many Omani men complete their costumes with traditional accessories, such as the walking stick, rifle, and the *khangar*—an elaborately carved dagger with a decorated hilt.

GEORG GERSTER

LIVING RESERVOIRS
SLAKE DESERT THIRST

A Bushman sips rainwater collected in a tree hollow. For about ten months each year, when no standing water exists in the central Kalahari, Bushmen gather bulbs, tubers, and melons—juicy plants that satisfy as much as 90 percent of their water needs. The Bushmen also obtain liquid by squeezing it from the stomachs of the animals they kill.

ROLAND AND SABRINA MICHAUD

ANCIENT WHEEL
WATERS CROPS

A scoop wheel, a primitive device employed for more than 2,000 years, helps a farmer irrigate his crops in the Turkestan Desert of Afghanistan.

A camel, hitched to a long wooden arm attached to a vertical shaft, slowly walks in a circle and turns the wheel. Cans tied to the rim dip into a stream, fill, and spill water onto a sluice that empties into an irrigation ditch.

This muscle-powered, water-lifting machine—introduced throughout the Middle East and parts of Europe by the Arabs during the Middle Ages—has allowed desert dwellers to turn otherwise unproductive acreage into fertile fields.

THOMAS J. ABERCROMBIE, NATIONAL GEOGRAPHIC STAFF

THE CAMEL:
A BEDOUIN'S BEST FRIEND

To the Bedouin in the deserts of the Middle East, camels have almost meant life itself. The animals, which can live on sparse thorny plants, provide meat and milk—sometimes the only food available in the desert—hair for cloth, and hides for saddles and sandals.

Broad, soft feet enable camels to carry heavy loads across loose sand. Conserving body moisture efficiently, the animals can cross vast arid tracts without needing water. The Bedouin have some 160 words for the indispensable animal, but they often simply call the camel "God's Gift."

PAUL CHESLEY

ROD BORLAND/BRUCE COLEMAN LTD.

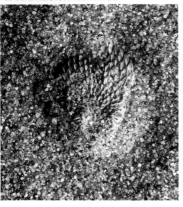

SNAKES SIDESTEP THE DESERT HEAT

The sidewinder rattlesnake of North America has developed an efficent way to move over sand. Instead of winding its body forward, the reptile (left) advances by looping its body sideways. It braces itself against the ground in only two or three spots, raising and shifting first one loop of its body, then another. This diagonal motion reduces slippage.

Desert vipers from other continents have also adopted the sidewinding technique. The sidewinder rattler hunts at dawn and at night to keep cool. But its distant relative (far left) in the Namib Desert of southwestern Africa can hunt during the day. It buries itself up to its eyes in sand and watches for prey.

ROD BORLAND/BRUCE COLEMAN INC.

ACROBATICS: A SPIDER'S TRICK

Legs folded, a "dancing white lady" spider of the Namib can escape an enemy by cartwheeling down a sand dune. The spider hides from predators by draping a web camouflaged with sand over its burrow. The development of such elaborate defenses reflects the fierce competition for limited food in the desert.

NATIONAL GEOGRAPHIC PHOTOGRAPHER BRUCE DALE

FLEET-FOOTED BIRD RACES FOR ITS DINNER

The roadrunner reaches speeds of up to 15 miles an hour in pursuit of prey. The bird can fly short distances, but its powerful legs and X-shaped feet make it a specialized runner. The speedster obtains water from food—mainly lizards, insects, and snakes.

Member of the cuckoo family, the roadrunner nests in trees, thorny shrubs, and cactuses in its desert habitat of the southwestern United States and northern Mexico. Black skin on its back absorbs solar radiation and helps keep the bird warm during cooler periods, such as the early morning hours.

ROD BORLAND/BRUCE COLEMAN INC. (BELOW, LEFT); EDWARD S. ROSS (BELOW, RIGHT)

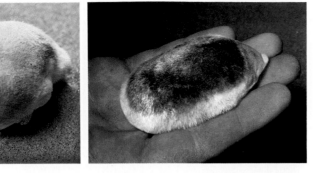

GOOD HEARING
HELPS BLIND BURROWERS

Suited for life underground, the Namib golden mole has strong claws for digging and a leathery nose to push sand away (left). At an early age, the animal's eyelids grow together, keeping sand out. Keen hearing helps the sightless burrower avoid danger and find food, such as an insect larva (far left).

NATIONAL GEOGRAPHIC PHOTOGRAPHER BATES LITTLEHALES

REPTILES MOVE
WITH THE SUN

Like all reptiles, lizards can regulate their body temperature by moving into and out of sunlight. A spiny lizard (left) faces into the midday sun, thus reducing heat gain by exposing less of its body surface to direct light. In cooler periods, the lizard lies at a right angle to the sun's rays, soaking up more warmth by increasing its exposure to the sun.

TOM MCHUGH

FISH AT HOME
IN THE DESERT

Since the last Ice Age, generations of pupfish have adapted to the extreme temperatures of isolated streams, springs, and pools of the American Southwest. These hardy fish can tolerate water that ranges from near freezing to more than 100°F.

NATIONAL GEOGRAPHIC PHOTOGRAPHER BRUCE DALE

FROG SAVES
ITS OWN SKIN

Like all amphibians, this South American frog absorbs and loses moisture through its skin. To endure long periods of drought, it retreats underground and produces a thin cocoon of dead skin that encloses it like plastic wrap and helps it retain body moisture. With rain, the frog sheds the skin and emerges to feed and breed in temporary pools. Its offspring bury themselves and await the next downpour.

CHARLES G. SUMMERS, JR.

SPECIALIZED FEATHERS
SOAK UP WATER

As a male sandgrouse drinks, it drenches its belly feathers, which sop up water. The bird returns to its nest, and chicks strip the wet feathers of every drop. The male has plumage more developed for holding water than has the female. Unlike birds that obtain moisture from their food, the sandgrouse subsists largely on a diet of dry seeds and must drink daily. It will fly 30 miles or more to a water hole.

Africa's desert heat can kill developing chicks in eggs left uncovered, so the parents take turns sitting on the nest. Only when one parent returns from drinking does the other leave to drink and feed.

Relatives of the pigeon, sandgrouses fly rapidly and can avoid all but the fastest predators, such as falcons. But sandgrouses risk attack when they stop to drink. Finding some protection in numbers, the birds usually travel in small flocks, but may congregate by the thousand at rivers and ponds (left). The birds drink rapidly and fly off, thus reducing their vulnerability to enemies on the ground.

M. P. KAHL/BRUCE COLEMAN INC.

M. P. L. FOGDEN/BRUCE COLEMAN INC.

A RODENT
THAT DOESN'T DRINK

The nocturnal kangaroo rat conserves moisture so efficiently that it does not have to drink at all. It can live on metabolic water produced from the dry food it eats.

KARL H. SWITAK

UNDERGROUND HAVENS
SHADE TURTLES

In the coolness of its burrow, a desert tortoise —like the kangaroo rat—escapes high temperatures at midday. A thick shell and armored skin insulate the animal and reduce water loss. Desert tortoises survive on metabolic water and on moisture contained in the food they eat. These reptiles can even store water in a large bladder for later use.

JEN & DES BARTLETT/BRUCE COLEMAN INC.

CACTUS OFFERS ROOM AND BOARD

Found in the Sonoran Desert where saguaros grow, elf owls nest in cactus holes drilled by Gila woodpeckers and flickers. Usually the owls move into abandoned homes in the cactuses, but occasionally the new boarders may evict the original occupants.

The great height of the saguaros, which can reach 50 feet, gives some protection from predators, and the fibrous cactus walls insulate the nest. Elf owl eggs hatch soon after the saguaros blossom in late spring. The creamy white flowers attract moths and other large insects, the main food of these nocturnal birds —the world's smallest owls.

GEORG GERSTER (ABOVE AND ABOVE, CENTER)

SOCIABLE WEAVERS SEEK PROTECTION IN NUMBERS

Sociable weavers in Africa build huge communal nests (left) that protect the birds from summer heat and winter cold.

The weavers construct their nests by thatching sticks and stems of grass on a branch. The size of the main nest increases as pairs of weavers add individual nest chambers under a huge domed roof (lower left). The larger the nest, the better the insulation and the more stable the temperature in occupied chambers.

In summer usually only two adult sociable weavers sleep in a chamber; the domed roof protects the birds from the hot sun. In winter four or five birds huddle in some of the nest chambers for warmth, leaving the other chambers empty. Thick nest walls hold in body heat, which helps keep the birds warm.

Acacia trees and drought-resistant aloes (upper left) provide the most suitable locations for the colonies. As an increasing number of telephone lines reach into the desert, the weavers use the poles for nest supports.

The birds live in the same place year-round. Squatters, such as pygmy falcons, often move into empty nest chambers and share the colony with the sociable weavers.

LONG-LEGGED BIRDS
OUTRUN DANGER

Flightless but fast, ostriches—the largest living birds—escape predators by stepping out at speeds as fast as 45 miles an hour. Long, loose feathers shield the birds from the heat and cold of Africa's deserts.

TOM NEBBIA-INC.

CLEM HAAGNER

LIZARDS TAKE REFUGE
HIGH AND LOW

Equipped with strong claws, an agamid lizard climbs bushes and trees to escape intense ground heat at midday in the Kalahari Desert of southern Africa (left). The reptile also uses its high perch as an observation post, surveying its surroundings for enemies and prey.

A sand-diving lizard (lower left) of Africa's Namib Desert retreats under the sand to keep cool. Toes fringed with elongated scales work like snowshoes to give the reptile traction, and a shovel-like snout helps it dig swiftly into the sand. These adaptations also enable the creature to evade enemies. Running at top speed, the sand-diving lizard can plunge headlong into loose sand and wriggle out of sight.

When the lizard grows too warm it raises its feet, legs, tail, and head to reduce body contact with the hot sand (lower left). This position exposes more skin surface to the air, allowing body heat to escape.

Other adaptations help lizards live in a world of sand. Some of the creatures have valve-like flaps to cover and protect their eyes and ears from sand as they burrow. Also, skin colors—yellows, red, and browns—blend with the arid surroundings and provide camouflage from predators.

ROD BORLAND

DAVID DE VRIES/BRUCE COLEMAN INC.

HEAT EXCHANGE
AIDS ANTELOPE

Too big to escape the heat by burrowing, the addax has adapted to endure it. The antelope's body temperature can reach 115°F before the animal begins to sweat and thereby lose valuable moisture.

A heat-exchange system prevents the addax's brain from overheating when the animal's body temperature rises. Veins that carry blood cooled in the nasal passages overlap a network of arteries carrying blood to the antelope's brain. The cooler venous blood lowers the temperature of the arterial blood and keeps heat from damaging the animal's brain.

The addax may wander hundreds of miles across the desert in search of food. It feeds after sundown when plants collect moisture from the cooler night air.

WARDENE WEISSER

LONG EARS DOUBLE
AS HEAT REGULATORS

The jackrabbit of North America avoids heat by seeking shelter in shady areas and in shallow, cool depressions in the ground.

Actually a hare, the jackrabbit uses its long ears to help regulate body temperature. When air temperature registers lower than the animal's body temperature, blood vessels in the ears dilate, allowing excess body heat to escape into the air. When outside temperatures rise higher than the hare's body temperature, blood vessels in the ears constrict to reduce heat gain from the environment. The large ears also enhance the jackrabbit's hearing.

SAVING FOOD
FOR A DUSTY DAY

Ballooning with nectar, these honey ants—called repletes—hang from the ceiling of a nest. Worker ants feed the repletes fluids obtained from plants and other insects. In droughts, the stored syrup sustains the colony.

NATIONAL GEOGRAPHIC PHOTOGRAPHER BRUCE DALE

GEORG GERSTER

SUCCULENTS HOARD PRECIOUS MOISTURE

Because desert perennial plants cannot avoid the drying glare of the sun, they have found other ways to withstand heat and water loss. Pulpy plants called succulents have large numbers of specialized cells that store water. Giant aloes (left) of Africa hoard water in thick, fleshy leaves and draw on the moisture in times of drought. Sunbirds sip nectar from the aloes' red blossoms and pollinate the flowers.

Except during the night or after a rain, succulents conserve water by keeping their pores closed. They take in carbon dioxide at night and convert it to an acid, which they store until daylight. Using energy from sunlight, the plants combine carbon dioxide and water to make carbohydrates—their food. This process, called photosynthesis, occurs in all green plants, but other plants open their pores during the day and do not store carbon dioxide for later use. During droughts, succulents may keep their pores closed for several months. The plants can continue photosynthesis by recycling carbon dioxide that forms when they use the carbohydrates they have manufactured.

MARTIN GROSNICK/ARDEA LONDON

SAGUAROS: NATURE'S WATER TOWERS

The fluted trunks and branches of saguaro cactuses (left) expand and contract like bellows in response to fluctuating amounts of stored moisture. The plants can store hundreds of gallons of water; thick waxy skins shield the moisture from the drying sun.

Cactuses, like all succulents, produce widespread shallow root systems to absorb rainwater before it evaporates. The absence of leaves reduces the surface area of the plant and decreases water loss. Spines help protect cactuses from browsing animals and help shade the plants from the sun.

Native to the Sonoran Desert, saguaros grow slowly and may take more than one hundred years to reach full height.

DAVID CAVAGNARO (BOTH)

AGAVES CLOSE UP
IN DROUGHT

During drought, when loss of water and food causes agave leaf bases to shrink, the leaves stand more upright, giving the plant a closed appearance (far left). In an open position (left) greater exposure of the leaves to sunlight speeds the plant's growth.

FRANS LANTING

WAX COATS SEAL OUT
RAYS OF THE SUN

A thick layer of wax on its stem protects the candelilla of North America by retaining moisture and reflecting light. Unrelated to cactuses, the succulent has similar desert adaptations. Its small surface area relative to its bulk reduces water loss and enables it to survive drier periods. Red blossoms appear in early spring and in late summer.

FRANS LANTING

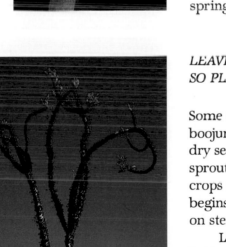

LEAVES DIE
SO PLANTS CAN LIVE

Some desert perennials, such as ocotillos and boojum trees, survive by shedding their leaves in dry seasons. After a rain the plants quickly sprout leaves. Each perennial may bear several crops of leaves annually, but when the plant begins to dry out, its leaves drop off. Waxy skin on stems and trunks seals in moisture.

Long, whiplike arms of the ocotillo (far left) support shiny oval leaves. When an ocotillo sheds its leaves, it goes into a state of reduced activity and minimal photosynthesis continues in the plant's stems. Leaf bases remain as sharp thorns and help repel browsing animals.

Boojums also become partially dormant when leafless and also retain their leaf bases as thorns (left). Their thick, gray-white bark offers protection from drying sunlight. The rare trees, which grow only in Baja California and Sonora, Mexico, store water in their tapering trunks and produce clusters of white flowers in late summer.

M.P.L. FOGDEN/BRUCE COLEMAN LTD.

GEORG GERSTER

LEAFY ARMS CATCH MOISTURE

Found only in the Namib Desert of southwestern Africa, *Welwitschia mirabilis* produces two leathery leaves in its lifetime.

They emerge from a carrotlike base and split and fray as they grow longer at rates of 4 to 8 inches each year. The straplike leaves collect moisture for the plant from the early morning fog that drifts across the Namib from the Atlantic coast.

Studies indicate that some of the largest *Welwitschia*—among the world's oldest plants— may have lived as long as 2,000 years.

NATIONAL GEOGRAPHIC PHOTOGRAPHER JAMES L. STANFIELD

SALTY SOIL HEALTHY FOR SOME PLANTS

When evaporation exceeds precipitation, salts tend to move upward through soil and accumulate near the surface. In these saline areas of the desert grow salt-tolerant plants called halophytes.

Researchers study halophytes hoping to develop food crops that can flourish on land too salty for conventional crops or that can live in fields irrigated with salt water. Samphire, a halophyte used in salads, blooms in an experimental field in Arizona (left).

RONALD F. THOMAS/BRUCE COLEMAN INC.

ROOTS DIG DEEP TO FIND WATER

A tree native to North America, the mesquite can grow long roots that tap moisture at great depths. The roots often reach 30 to 50 feet into the ground, but they may extend as deep as 175 feet. Some mesquites have only shallow root systems that drain moisture within a wide radius, limiting the growth of other trees in that area.

After a mesquite seed germinates, a taproot develops rapidly. Only after it locates a reliable water supply does the rest of the plant begin to grow significantly.

WALTER RAWLINGS/ROBERT HARDING PICTURE LIBRARY

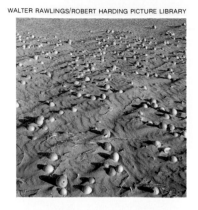

VINES ANCHOR
DESERT GOURDS

Hard-shelled gourds—fruits of plants called cucurbits—house seeds in the hot, dry Sahara. Mice and other small mammals sometimes gnaw the gourds open and help scatter the seeds. With sufficient moisture, the seeds sprout, often in hollows or gullies where rainfall collects. These plants belong to the same family as pumpkins and cucumbers.

GEORG GERSTER

MOISTURE WORKS
MIRACLES IN THE DESERT

With an inch of rain, the desert blooms. Lilies in Africa's Kalahari Desert flower quickly (left). During a drought, they exist underground as bulbs that store food and water. Ephemerals, such as wild primroses (below), sprout only when they have enough moisture. In lives that span just a few weeks, ephemerals produce hundreds of seeds. Like all desert life, the plants make the most of very little.

PETER L. KRESAN

Notes on Contributors

Tor Eigeland is a free-lance writer and photographer formerly based in Beirut, Lebanon. He has covered the Middle East for 20 years and has previously photographed Bedouin life for the Special Publication *Nomads of the World*. His assignments for other Special Publications include the Tarahumara Indians in *Primitive Worlds* and the Italian ranges in *The Alps*. Born in Norway, Eigeland now lives in Spain.

Dr. Farouk El-Baz is the Director of the Center for Earth and Planetary Studies at the Smithsonian Institution's National Air and Space Museum, in Washington, D.C. A geologist and an expert on arid lands, he uses space imagery to study world deserts. During the Apollo space program, Dr. El-Baz helped train astronauts in geology and photography, and he participated in the selection of sites for man's lunar landings. Dr. El-Baz learned to appreciate arid terrain early in life. He was born and raised in Egypt, a land 96 percent desert. Dr. El-Baz served as science adviser to President Anwar Sadat.

Photographer *Georg Gerster* holds a doctorate in German language and literature and English literature from the University of Zurich. For six years he served as science editor for the Swiss weekly *Weltwoche*. He began his career as a writer, taking up photography as a way to illustrate his texts. Today Gerster is considered one of the world's foremost aerial photographers. He is the author-photographer of 15 books, including *Grand Design*, *Brot und Salz—Bread and Salt*, and *Churches in Rock*. His work has also appeared in GEO magazine, the London *Sunday Times Magazine*, NATIONAL GEOGRAPHIC, and several of the Society's books.

The career of *Loren McIntyre* spans 35 years of writing, photography, filmmaking, and foreign service in South America. He has written and taken photographs for nine NATIONAL GEOGRAPHIC articles. He is the author and photographer of the Special Publication *The Incredible Incas and Their Timeless Land* and has contributed to many other Society publications. In 1971 McIntyre directed a Society-supported expedition that pinpointed the most distant source of the Amazon.

Avid outdoorsman *Tom Melham* has rowed the Colorado River, hiked the Grand Canyon, and explored coral reefs around the world during his 11 years of assignments for the Society. A native of Milwaukee, Melham has traveled extensively through the American West. The Special Publications senior writer is the author of *John Muir's Wild America*.

Since joining the Society in 1976, Special Publications senior writer *Thomas O'Neill* has retraced the routes of pathfinder John Frémont for *Into the Wilderness*, traveled the Southwest for *America's Majestic Canyons*, and journeyed to the ancient city of Pompeii for *Splendors of the Past*. He is the author of the Special Publication *Back Roads America*.

Born in Utah, *Joyce Stewart* lived for six years in Africa, where she returned on assignment for *The Desert Realm*. Now based in Washington, D.C., she works as a free-lance writer, editor, and translator specializing in psychiatry, ethology, and anthropology. She contributed to the two-volume Special Publication *National Geographic Book of Mammals*.

Acknowledgments

The Special Publications Division is grateful to the individuals and organizations named or quoted in the text and to those cited here for their generous cooperation and assistance during the preparation of this book: Bureau of Reclamation; Embassy of the Sultanate of Oman; International Center for Language Studies; The Ludwig Keimer Foundation for Comparative Research in Archaeology and Ethnology; State Alluvial Diggings; and Anthony Ashworth, C. G. Bohn, Carol S. Breed, William H. Brooks, Martha Ames Burgess, Tony L. Burgess, John L. Cloudsley-Thompson, Nicholas E. Collias, Ronald I. Crombie, Basil Davidson, Albert E. Dien, Mark Dimmitt, George E. Ericksen, Bernard L. Fontana, Barney Foran, Stefane Groueff, Stephen A. Halkovic, Thomas R. Howell, Kenneth S. Inglis, James V. Knight, H. E. Landsberg, Peter K. Latz, Roberta Lipson, Laurence J. C. Ma, William G. McGinnies, Park S. Nobel, Patricia Paylore, John E. Peterson, Troy L. Péwé, Eric R. Pianka, Geoff Pickup, Georg Petersen, Ulrich Petersen, Julian Rhinehart, Mary Seely, Knut Schmidt-Nielsen, R. H. Tedford, Myrna Tonkinson, A. S. Walker, George E. Watson.

Additional Reading

The reader may want to consult the *National Geographic Index* for related articles and to refer to the following books: Anthony Bannister and Peter Johnson, *Namibia* and *Okavango*; Alec Campbell, *The Guide to Botswana*; Jack Chen, *The Sinking Story*; J. L. Cloudsley-Thompson, *The Desert* and *Man and the Biology of Arid Zones*; René Gardi, *Blue Veils, Red Tents*; Richard A. Gould, *Yiwara Foragers of the Australian Desert*; Peter Hopkirk, *Foreign Devils on the Silk Road*; Robert Lacey, *The Kingdom: Arabia and the House of Saud*; Peggy Larson, *Deserts of America*; William G. McGinnies, *Discovering the Desert*; William G. McGinnies, Bram J. Goldman, Patricia Paylore, eds., *Deserts of the World*; Richard F. Nyrop, and others, *Area Handbook for the Persian Gulf States* and *Area Handbook for Saudi Arabia*; M. P. Petrov, *Deserts of the World*; Reader's Digest Atlas of Australia*; Knut Schmidt-Nielsen, *Desert Animals*; David Sheridan, *Desertification of the United States*; Frederic H. Wagner, *Wildlife of the Deserts*; Alf Wannenburgh, *The Bushmen*.

Index

Boldface indicates illustrations; *italic* refers to picture legends (captions).

Abdulaziz Al Saud, King (Saudi Arabia) 192, *195*
Aboriginals 251, 253, **254-255**, 256, **256**, 257, **257**, *264-265*, 268, 282; cave painting **252**; hunting 253, 256, 257; mythology *248*, 257, 258
Acacia (tree): Australia 250; Niger **138**
Adaptation, desert life 30, 284; animal, *290-295*; human, *284-289*; plant, *296-299*
Addax 295, **295**
Adobe architecture *284*, **284**
aflaj (water distribution system) *202*, 202, **202**, *216*
African jacana (bird) **171**
Agamid lizard *294*, **294**
Agave 65, *297*, **297**
Ahaggar Mountains, Algeria 112
Ajo Range, Ariz. **64**
Alice Springs, Australia 250-251, 253, **266-267**, 272, *276*
Al Jabal Al Akhdar (mountain), Oman **200-201**
Aloe *293*, *296*, **296**
Altiplano (plain), Bolivia 78, 90, **92, 93**
Anasazi 73, *287*
Anchovies 96, 97, *102*; commercial fishing 97, *102*
Andado Station (ranch), Australia 269, 272, **274-275**, *276*, **277**
Andagua valley, Peru: cinder cones **88-89**
Andes (mountain chain), South America **6-7**, 79, **82-83, 88-89, 90-91, 98-99**; irrigation tunnels 100-101
Aporosaura anchietae see sand-diving lizard
Arabian Peninsula: map 187
Arabs 10, 186; Saharan commerce 128; *see also* Bedouin
Aridity index: defined 14-21
Atacama Desert, Chile 76-109; aridity index 14; map 79

Atakor (mountain range), Algeria **118-119**
Atkins, Joe 282
Australia 248-283; land reclamation **278-279**; livestock **274, 275**; map 251; pastoralists 268-269, *275, 278*; natives *see* Aboriginals
Ayers Rock, Australia **3, 248-249**; Aboriginal mythology *248, 258*

badgirs (wind towers) *32*
Bagnold, Ralph 21, 22
Bahariya Oasis, Egypt **144**
Baluchi nomads: tents *286*, **286**
Barchan dunes **24, 145**; cause *24*
Basin and range: Nevada *62, 69*
Bedouin 21, 120, 186-187, **188, 189**, 192, 207, 208, 212, 213, **213**; camels *28, 289*, **289**; customs 187, *188*, 192, *284*, **284**; herders **212**; name origin 203
Beja (people): caravans 128-129
Benguela Current: aridity caused by 14, *151, 163, 175*
Beni Isguen, Algeria 129, 131
Big Bend National Park, Texas **44-45**
Bonneville Salt Flats, Utah **62**
Boojum trees **54**, *297*, **297**
Bou Noura, Algeria **121**, 129
Buddhist shrines: China **222**, *223*, *223*, 230
Bunchgrass **97**
Bushmen **42-43**, *148*, 150, 151, **152-153**, *154*, **180-181**, 182, *288*, **288**, *289*, **289**

Cabbage palms **271**
Cactuses: dune stabilization **16, 17**; range *52-53*; *see also* individual species
California poppies **64**
Camels **4**, 186-187, 272, 289, **289**; Bactrian **36, 37**; caravan use 128; meat 194, *289*; milk 187, *289*; racing **28-29**
Campbell, Alexander Colin 154
Candelilla (plant) 68, *297*, **297**
Canyonlands National Park, Utah 69, 72; The Needles, **62-63**
Caravans 128; decline 121; Mauritania 131, *132*; Niger **136-137**, *139*; restrictions 121, *135*; trails 128, 230
Cardon cactuses **54**, *97*
Casuarina trees: dune stabilization

16, 17
Central Arizona Project (water diversion system) 65, **68**, *69*, **69**
Chalk pillar: Egypt **143**
Chihuahuan Desert, Mexico–U. S. *44*, **44-45**, 46, *47*; map *47*; plants 46
Chile 76-109; irrigation **83, 84-85**; mining *104*, **104, 105**; salitre 95-96; volcanoes **88**, 90
China 218-247; agriculture 223, *226*, **227**, 231, **238-239**, 240; communes *224*, 240; dune stabilization 224; *see also* Gobi; Taklimakan
Chinguetti, Mauritania 131, **132**
Chipaya Indians **93**; sod huts **92**
Chisos Mountains, Texas **44-45**
Cholla cactus 65
Chuquicamata, Chile: copper mine **83**, 90, 94, tailings **104**
Clark family 269, 272, **277**; ranch *see* Andado Station
Cliff dwellings: Mesa Verde, Colo. **287**, *287*
Colca, Río (river), Peru: irrigation use 101
Colorada, Laguna (playa), Bolivia **76-77**
Colorado Plateau, U. S. 69, 73; formation 69, 72
Colorado River, Mexico–U. S. **74-75**; water diversion 65, **68**, *69*, **69**, *71*, 72
Cooke, H. J. 150, 154
Cooling systems, passive *18*, 30, *32*, **32, 33**
Cormorants **102, 103**
Couëlle, Jacques 120-121
Cucurbits: gourds *299*, **299**

Dahash, Anbar 207
Dakhla Oasis, Egypt **145**
"dancing white lady" spider *290*, **290**
Dasht-e Kavir, Iran 21, *215*; aerial view **214**; map 187
Dasht-e Lut, Iran **214-215**; map 187
Date palms **122-125**, *146*, *202*
Death Valley, Calif. 46, 48, 52, **56, 57**
Desalinization plants: Saudi Arabia 194, **195**
Desert tortoise *292*, **292**
Devil's Golf Course, Calif. **56-57**

Dhows (boats) **198**
Diamond mining: Namibia 163, **174, 175,** *176*
"The Dragon" (dune), Chile *39,* **40-41**
the Dreaming (Aboriginal mythology) 254, 257-258
Druid Arch, Utah 72
Dry farming: Anasazi *287;* Hopi 39, **59, 60-61**
Dumont Sand Dunes, Calif. **53**
Dune stabilization 223-224; China 224, *243,* **243;** India 27, 30; Somalia **16, 17**
Dunes: formation 26; movement *16,* 26, 27, rate 27; sounds made 243; types 24, **24, 25,** 27, **27,** 242; world's highest *161*
Dust storms: Australia **266-267,** 269, 272

Egypt: tomb mural *14,* **14;** *see also* Western Desert
El Golea, Algeria 121
El Harra, Egypt: well **144**
El Hart, Morocco **126-127;** perfume industry *127*
El Niño (current) 97, *102*
El Oued, Algeria: market **125;** palm groves **124-125**
El Qasr, Egypt **15**
Elephants **168**
Elf owl *293,* **293**
Ellström, Nils 101
Empty Quarter, Arabian Peninsula *see* Rub al-Khali
Emu **252;** cave painting **252**
Eremophila (shrub) **283**
Erosion 10, 22, 26, *52, 57, 61,* 65, 69, 72, **86-87,** *141,* **142-143,** *161,* 208, *278*
Etosha National Park, Namibia 155, 158; pans **167, 168, 169;** springs 158, 159; wildlife 158-159, **168-169**
Eyre, Lake, Australia 250; mythology 258

Fa Xian: quoted *233*
Fahd, Crown Prince (Saudi Arabia) **195**
Farafra Oasis, Egypt 22
Faraj, Abdullah 207, 208
Farm 150 (commune), China 240
Fathy, Hassan 30
Felger, Richard S. 65, 68
Fertilizer *see* Guano deposits;

Salitre
Fish: desert pools 120, *167, 291,* **291;** subterranean 121
Fishing: Oman **198,** *199,* 203, *285*
Flash floods: deserts 46, *66,* 94, **94**
Frankincense *30,* **31**
Fulani (people) **130,** *131*
Fur seals **101**
"Fuzzy-Wuzzy" *see* Beja

Gaochang (ruins), China **228**
Gemsbok 158, **160, 168-169**
Ghardaïa, Algeria **110-111,** 129, 131
Gibson, Everett 22
Gibson Desert, Australia 250; Aboriginals 253, **254-255;** map 251
Gila monster **65**
Giles, Ernest 258, 268; quoted 268, *269*
Glubb, John Bagot (Glubb Pasha) 203
Goatherds **115, 212**
Gobabeb, Namibia: research institute 159-160; annual precipitation 175
Gobi (desert), Asia *220,* 221; formation 223; name meaning *220,* 221; map 220
Goldsworthy Mining Limited, Australia 273, 282
Goniatites (fossils) 112, **128, 129**
Gould, Richard 253
Great Basin, U. S. 46, *47,* 69; plants 46; map 47
Great Indian Desert, India **18-19,** *286;* inhabitants **18, 19,** 27; Landsat image **20;** map 13
Great Sand Sea, Egypt 21, *141*
Great Sandy Desert, Australia 250; Landsat image **262-263;** map 251
Great Wall of China 223, 230, **236, 237**
Guano deposits 78, 96-97, *102*
Guayule 68-69
Gurbantünggüt Desert, China 221; communes 240; map 220

Halophytes, *298,* **298**
Hassan Abdullah al-Murrassa 195, 202
Hedin, Sven Anders 240, 242
High Atlas Mountains, Morocco **127**
Hitchcock, Robert K. 150, 154

Hogans (Navajo shelters) *287,* **287**
Honey ants *295,* **295**
Hopi: desert agriculture 39, **59, 60-61**
Hotan, China 234, **244, 245**
Humboldt, Alexander von *5,* 78
Humboldt Current *see* Peru Current
Humboldt penguins **100**
Hydroelectric power: China 234, reservoir **235**

Imperial Valley, Calif.: irrigation 65, **70-71,** salt buildup 65, *71*
Incas 7; shrines 90
Indians of North America: animism 48; wild foods 59, 65; *see also* individual tribes
Institute of Desert Research, China 224, **242**
Iran: architecture **32, 33;** irrigation system **216, 217**
Islam (religion) 10, *188, 189,* **190-191,** 192, 231, 240, *244*
Israel 212-213; desert farming **208, 209**

Jabbaren, Algeria 113
Jackrabbit 30, *295,* **295**
Jaisalmer, India *286,* **286**
Jericho **210-211;** ancient city *211*
Jiayuguan (fortress), China 230, **236, 237**
Jojoba 68, **208,** 213
Jordan 203-212
Joshua trees 46, 52

Kalahari Desert, Africa *148,* 150-151, 154, **172, 180-183;** dry season *289;* map 151; Okavango Delta **170-171;** wildlife *151,* 155, **164-165**
Kangaroo rat *292,* **292**
Kashi, China 224, 230; rug merchant **225**
Kerzaz, Algeria **115, 122-123**
Khalid, King (Saudi Arabia) **195**
Kharga basin, Egypt: dune movement 27
Khutse Game Reserve, Botswana: pan **183**
Kimber, Richard 253, 272, 282
Kipling, Rudyard 128
Klopper, Donald 163
Kolmanskop, Namibia **176, 177**
Kuiseb River, Namibia **156-157,**

159, **159**; floods **158**

Lancaster, Nick 160, 163
Landsat images: desert research
  21; California, southern **49**;
  Chile **82-83, 91**; Egypt **141**; Great
  Indian Desert, India **20**; Great
  Sandy Desert, Australia **262-263**;
  Lop Nur (dry lake), China **241**;
  Namib Desert, Africa **156-157**;
  Rub al-Khali, Arabian Peninsula
  193; Turpan Depression, China
  228-229
Lanzhou, China 224, *237*, *243*
Lawrence, T. E. 21, 208
Lejia, Laguna (salar), Chile **34-35**
Lilies *299*, **299**
Linear dunes *26*, **156-157**
Llama **84**
Loa, Río (river), Chile 79, **83-84**
Loess soil: China 223
Lop Nur (dry lake), China 240,
  240, **241**, 242

Mabbutt, Jack 250
Macdonnell Ranges, Australia **270-
271**
Majes Project, Peru 100-101
Makgadikgadi Pans, Botswana
  155, **172-173**; wildlife *172*
Mandara, Lake, Libya **8-9**
María Elena (salitre plant), Chile
  96
Mauritania: drought 131, *132*;
  population 132; women 132
Mesquite 67, *100*, *298*, **298**; beans
  68
Middle East 184-217; changes in
  life-style *184*, 213; map 187;
  petroleum production *184*;
  traditional dress 194-195, *288*
Mills, Clive and Thelma 282
Mingsha (sand mound), China:
  sounds made 243
Mojave Desert, U. S. *47*, *52*, **57**;
  floods *57*; map *47*; plants 46
Mongolian People's Republic:
  nomads *36-37*, *37*, *246*, **246, 247**
Mozabites **110-111**, *121*, 129, 131
Murals: Buddhist shrine *223*, **223**
Murphy, Robert Cushman 97
Muslims *188*; pilgrims **190-191**;
  prayers *188*, **189**
Myers, Fred 253, 256
M'zab (oasis region), Algeria *110*,
  121, 129, 131; population 129

Nabateans *207*, 208, 212
Namib Desert, Africa 14, **148-149,
  151, 158**, 159, **159-162**, *177*;
  diamond mining 163, **174-175,**
  176; fog *43*, **148-149**, *151*, **162,**
  175; map 151
Namib golden mole *291*, **291**
Namib Research Institute,
  Gobabeb, Namibia **159**, 159-160
Navajo **58**, *59*, 69; hogans *287*, **287**
Nazca lines (figure tracings), Peru
  100, **108, 109**
Nazwa, Oman **202**; market *285*,
  285
Negev Desert, Israel: agriculture
  208, 209, 212-213; map 187
Nelson, Jock 269
North American deserts 44-75;
  animals 47, *65*; botanical
  division 46; drownings 46; map
  47; plants 46, 47
Nouakchott, Mauritania 131-132,
  133

ORVs **52, 53**
Ocotillo (plant) *297*, **297**
oficinas (nitrate plants) 96, **104-
105**
Oil tankers **196-197**
Okavango Delta, Botswana 155,
  170, 171
Olgas, Australia **264-265**
Oman 194-203; agriculture 195,
  200-201, 202; development 195,
  202, 203; irrigation 202, *202*,
  202, 203; fishing **198**, *199*, 203,
  285; petroleum industry *197*,
  202-203; traditional dress 194-
  195, *288*, **288**
Orange River, Africa 159, 163
Ostriches 159, *167*, *294*, **294**

Paciencia, Llano de la (plains),
  Chile 90; flash flood **94**
Pan American Highway, South
  America 79, 90, **109**
Papago Indians 53, 59
Parra Hake, Heriberto 65, 68
Pasternak, Dov 212-213
Peru 76-109; dunes, coastal **106-
107**; guano deposits 78, 96-97,
  102; livestock *98*, **98-99**
Peru Current: aridity caused by 14,
  78; *El Niño*, effects of 97, *102*
Peruvian Desert, Peru 76-109;
  aridity index 14; map 79

Petra (ancient city), Jordan **206-
207**, 208, 212
Petroleum industry: Middle East
  184, 186, 192, **196**, *197*, 213
Playas (evaporated lakes) 48, **57,
  76-77, 214**
Polar deserts 10, 22, **22**; map 13
Polo, Marco: quoted 243
Poplar trees **226-227**, 242
Prickly pear cactus **44-45**
Primroses *299*, **299**
Pupfish *291*, **291**

Qaboos bin Said, Sultan (Oman)
  195
qanats (irrigation system) **216,
217**
Qara, Egypt **146-147**
Qattara Depression, Egypt 21, *112*,
  119, 144, 146-147
Quebrada Camiña (river valley),
  Chile **83, 84-85**
quinua (grain) *93*, **93**

Racetrack (playa), Calif.: moving
  rocks 48, *52*, **57**
Rachewiltz, Boris de 128-129
Reiche, Maria 100, **109**
Roadrunner (bird) *290*, **290**
Rocha, Orlando 94
Rock paintings: Botswana 154,
  154, 155; Sahara 113, 114,
  periods 114
Rocks, moving 48, 52, **57**
Rohlfs, Gerhard 21
Royal Jordanian Desert Police 203,
  204, 205, *207*, 208, **284**
Rub al-Khali, Arabian Peninsula
  21, **184-185**, 186, *187*; map 187;
  petroleum exploration 186
Rum, Wadi, Jordan **204-205**, 207-
208

Sacred Mosque, Mecca, Saudi
  Arabia *189*, **190-191**; seizure 192
Saguaro cactuses **1, 38**, 46, 53, 59,
  66-67, *293*, *296*, **296**; flower **39**
Sahara (desert), Africa 110-147;
  aridity index 14, 21; climatic
  changes 27, 112, 113, 114;
  landforms 112-113, *113*, *114*;
  map 113; name meaning 112,
  113;
Salitre 95-96, *104*; processing
  plants 96, abandoned **104-105**
Salt trade **4-5**, 128, **135, 136-137**

Samphire (plant) *298*, **298**
San (people) *see* Bushmen
San Pedro de Atacama, Chile *90, 94*
Sanchez, Roberto 94
Sand-diving lizard 163, *294*, **294**
Sand goanna (lizard) **256**
Sand seas 21; defined 26-27
Sand snake **146**
Sandgrouses *292*, **292**
Saudi Arabia 186-194; development 192, 194, *195*; foreign workers 192; petroleum industry 192, *195*; water supply 194; women 192
Schrager, Stanley N. 131
Sea lions **101**
Seabirds *102*, **102-103**; *see also* Guano deposits
Secretary bird **168**
Seely, Mary 160, *175*
Seif dunes **24, 40-41, 133,** cause 24
Sekaquaptewa, Eugene 39
Shay Gap (town), Australia 273, 282
Sidewinding snakes *290*, **290**
Silk Road, Asia *218*, 224-230, *224*, 231, *233, 237, 240;* oases 224-230
Simpson Desert, Australia 250, **260-261;** map 251
Siwa (oasis), Egypt 11, **140-141**
Sodium nitrate *see* Salitre
Sodium sulfate *104*, **104**
Solar energy: experimental power plant **50-51;** housing **48,** *287,* **287**
Somalia: dune stabilization **16, 17**
Sonoran Desert, Mexico–U. S. *1,* 47, **66-67;** aridity index 21; flash floods **66;** map *47;* plants 46, cactuses *1,* 53, **54, 66-67**
Sossusvlei, Namibia **160,** 161
South American deserts 76-109; map *79; see also* Atacama Desert; Peruvian Desert
Spinifex 250, 268, **271**
Spinifex hopping-mouse **282**
Spiny lizard *291,* **291**
Springbok 159, **164-165, 168-169**
Star dunes **24-25, 157,** 161; causes *24*
Stations (ranches): Australia 268-269, 272, **274-277**
Stein, Aurel 230
Stewart, Ian 282
Stuart, John McDouall 268

Sturt, Charles *258*
Sturt Stony Desert, Australia 250, **259;** map 251
Sturt's desert pea 251, **282**
Succulents (plants) *296*, **296**

Taklimakan Desert, China *220, 221,* 230, **231, 234,** 242-243; pyramid dunes 27; map *220;* ruins in **232-233**
Tamanrasset, Algeria 112, 128
Tassili-n-Ajjer (plateau), Algeria: rock art 113-114, **116-117**
Tatio geyser field, Chile **88**
Taylor Valley, Antarctica **22**
Tenebrionid beetle **163**
Ténéré Desert, Niger **138, 139,** map 113
Tengger Desert, China 223-224, **243;** map 220
Tian Shan (mountains), China **226-227;** Landsat image **228-229**
Tipton, Jimmy 69
Todd River, Australia 251, *266*
Transverse dunes **156-157**
Tsodilo Hills, Botswana 154; rock paintings 154, **154, 155**
Tuareg (people) **5,** 114, *118,* 120-121, **139;** caravan **136-137;** salt buyer **135;** women 120
Tucson, Ariz.: solar housing *287,* **287**
Turpan Depression, China *226,* **228-229,** 240

Uygurs *224,* **225, 227, 228, 231,** 240, **244, 245**

"Valley of the Moon," Chile 94, **94**
Volcanoes: South America *88-89,* **88,** 90

War of the Pacific 95
Ward, John 160, 163

Weavers, sociable (birds) *293,* **293;** nests **293**
"The Weeping Gate", Great Wall, China 231
Welwitschia mirabilis 175, *298,* **298**
Western Desert, Egypt 10; exploration 21, motor vehicle use 21-22; irrigation **145;** map 113
Wildebeests **168-169**
Willow bushes *231,* **242**
World: map 12-13

Xau, Lake, Botswana 155
Xinjiang Uygur Autonomous Region, China 223, 230, 231, *234, 244*

Yardangs (wind eroded rocks) 26, **26,** 242; word origin 242
Yellen, John E. 154
Yellow River, China 223, **242**
Yin Shan gorge, China **218-219**
Yucca 46, **65**

Zhao Songqiao 221-223, 243
Zhu Zhenda 224, 242

Library of Congress CIP **Data**
Main entry under title:
The Desert realm.

  Bibliography: p.
  Includes index.
  1. Deserts. 2. Desert ecology.
I. National Geographic Society (U. S.). Special Publications Division.
GB611.D395   508.315'4   80-7568
                                        AACR2
ISBN 0-87044-331-3 (regular binding)
ISBN 0-87044-456-5 (library binding)

Composition for *The Desert Realm: Lands of Majesty and Mystery* by Composition Systems Inc., Arlington, Va., and National Geographic's Photographic Services (index pages). Printed and bound by Holladay-Tyler Printing Corp., Rockville, Md. Color separations by The Lanman Progressive Co., Washington, D. C.; Lincoln Graphics, Inc., Cherry Hill, N.J.; and Nashville Electragraphics, Inc., Nashville, Tenn.

NATIONAL GEOGRAPHIC magazine makes an ideal gift for any occasion. For information about membership in the National Geographic Society, call 800-638-4077, toll free, or write to the National Geographic Society, Dept. 1675, Washington, D. C. 20036.